Hebrew

Maccabees

(The Book of the Hammer)

SCRIPTURAL RESEARCH INSTITUTE
Published by Digital Ink Productions, 2024

Copyright

Hebrew Maccabees

First edition. March 11, 2024

Copyright © 2024 Scriptural Research Institute.

ISBN: 978-1-998288-67-0

Hebrew Maccabees was composed in Hebrew between 418 and 439 AD. This English translation was created by the Scriptural Research Institute in 2024.

The image used for the cover is an artistic reinterpretation of 'Victorious Hannibal views Italy from the Alps' by Francisco Goya, painted in 1771. The original painting is in the Prado Museum, in Madrid.

Table of Contents

TABLE OF CONTENTS

Forward

Hebrew Maccabees is one of the stranger Hebrew books to have survived to the present and is either a relic of the oldest surviving book about Judas the Hammer, or a remarkably heretical medieval forgery. There is no academic consensus on what it is, and few scholars have bothered to comment on it. The book deals with the life of Judas 'the Maccabee,' which is of little interest to Christians. His life is of interest to Jews, however, almost all books dealing with the Maccabean Revolt are rejected as scripture in Rabbinical Judaism. Jews generally treat the Septuagint's 1st and 2nd Maccabees, and Josephus' *Antiquities of the Judeans* as historical texts of debatable accuracy, while using the *Megillat Taanit* and *Megillat Antiochus* as sources on how Hanukkah should be practiced. Hanukkah, also called the Festival of Lights, is a holiday based on the rededication of the temple in Jerusalem that happened when Judas occupied Jerusalem. The festival continues, but all records of what happened are lost or ignored.

The *Megillat Taanit* dates to the 1st century AD, and the *Megillat Antiochus* dates to the 2nd century AD, and neither is considered a historically reliable source by academics. This suggests that what actually happened in the time of Judas was actively suppressed during the Hasmonean and Herodian dynasties, likely because Judas was later viewed as a heretic. In most of the books featuring Judas, he reports seeing angelic horsemen that no one else could see. These horsemen are clearly part of Judas' story, however, if they were, in fact, angels riding horses, then Judas would be a prophet. Yet, he is not accepted as a prophet in Judaism or Christianity.

The idea of angels riding horses is itself unheard of in Israelite and Judahite texts, other than in texts related to Judas, which suggests he may have actually been following a different religion. During the era of the Maccabean Revolt, the high priest in Jerusalem was not a Judahite, but a Phrygian named Philip. The Phrygians worshiped Sabazdiôs (ϨΑ8ΑϮΧΟϨ), the great horseman of the sky, who was represented by a hand. The Greeks interpreted the Phrygian Sabazios (Σαβάζιος) and Judahite Sabaoth (Σαβαώθ) as two forms of Dionysus (Διόνῡσος). In *2nd Maccabees*, Dionysus is used as the name of the god worshiped in the temple in Jerusalem under Greek rule. Sabaoth was recorded by the Greeks of the Hellenistic era as the name of the Judahite god, based on the Aramaic ṣbåwt (צבאות), meaning 'desires.' However, this word took on a very different meaning as Classical Hebrew formed during the Maccabean Revolt, becoming a word meaning 'armies' or 'battles.'

The duel meanings of 'ṣbåwt' in Semitic languages go back to very ancient times, where the oldest recorded form was the Akkadian sābum (𒍢), meaning 'soldier.'

2

Over thousands of years, the name transitioned to 'server' and finally 'desires' in Aramaic and 'abundance' (صبا) in Arabic. When the Hasmonean dynasty decided to 'restore' the Hebrew language, many ancient words and meanings were introduced to the Judahite dialect of Canaanite, resulting in the new Hebrew language having many archaic terms, including ṣbåwt (צבאות). The name Sabaoth (Σαβαώθ) is used in the Septuagint, generally where the Masoretic texts used the word 'armies' (צבאות), which has resulted in many modern academics simply accepting this as a mistranslation, however, in *Hebrew Maccabees*, Judas is repeatedly referred to as the 'Anointed of Sabaoth,' confirming that if nothing else, the author viewed Sabaoth as a proper god.

While it is natural to assume that the Maccabean Revolt was about getting rid of the worship of Sabaoth / Sabazios / Dionysus, as recounted in *2^(nd) Maccabees*, this book contradicts that, and reports that Judas was a Sabaoth worshiper. Moreover, there is some incidental evidence of the continuation of Sabaoth worship under the rule of the Hasmoneans in the writing of Josephus, and also the Babylonian Talmud. *2^(nd) Maccabees* reports that when Philip was the high priest, the Dionysia was celebrated in Jerusalem. The Dionysia was a Greek festival celebrating the rebirth of Dionysus, in the equivalent of the Gregorian month of March.

The City Dionysia festival of the ancient Greek city-states took place anywhere between the 10th and 16th of the month of Elaphêboliôn (Ἐλαφηβολιών), depending on the city-state. The Greek calendar of the era was also lunisolar, and so the Dionysia could fall anywhere in late March. Worshippers of Dionysus were required to drink until they did not know good from evil. In Rome, the festival was known as the Bacchanalia and happened sometime in March before the adoption of the Julian Calendar, and then on March 17. The Bacchanalia was a festival in which worshippers of Bacchus became drunk and used various drugs. According to Roman records, the name of the Judean god was Bacchius Judaeus (BACCHIVS IVDAEUS), meaning Bacchus of Judea. Dionysis was viewed as being the Greek Bacchus, Sabazdiôs the Phrygian Bacchus, and the sacred bull Buchis (ⲃⲩⲩⲱϩ) as the Egyptian version.

The syncretic cult likely began in Egypt under the rule of the last Pharaoh, Nectanebo II, who reigned between 358 and 340 BC. His kingdom of Egypt fought a series of defensive wars against Persia, ultimately being defeated just a decade before Alexander would conquer them. The Buchis bull ceremony, like the older Apis bull ceremony, was a celebration of spirit (kå) and rebirth which took place in the spring. However, the Buchis bull was viewed as the incarnation of Monthu, the god of war, unlike the Apis bull, which was viewed as the incarnation of the Nile god Hapi. Both the Bachis bull and the Apis bull were also viewed as messengers of Osiris, the god of rebirth, as the ceremonies took place in the springtime when the world seemed to be reborn. Nectanebo II's reason for making the cult was likely because he was heavily reliant on foreign mercenaries, especially Greeks, Phrygians, Thracians, and Canaanites, and this cult merged many of their common religious elements, however, this god was not enough to protect Egypt from Persia.

In the 2nd century BC, the Roman Senate became concerned about the influence the cult of Bacchus was exerting over Rome, and various political assassinations were linked to the cult. In 186 BC, the Roman Senate wrote laws to restrict the cult and merged the worship of Bacchus with the older Latin god of wine Liber Pater.

The Judean Dionysia does not appear to have ended by the time the author wrote *Hebrew Maccabees*, as the author recorded the following near the end of Judas' life:

Ever since that time, the Judeans celebrate this day as a feast and a holiday, on which wine is drunk on the 13th day of Adar, one day before Purim.

This is not related to any Rabbinical festival, as the 13th day of Adar is the Fast of Esther, not a day of feasting. The Purim holiday customs have developed since the era that the Babylonian Talmud was compiled to include funny costumes and parades, however, this does not reflect the Purim of the Talmudic era. The Fast of Esther is accepted as originating in Babylonia during the Geonic period, broadly dated to between 589 and 1038 AD. The Geonic period was the era that immediately followed the Talmudic era, when the Geons of the two great Babylonian Talmudic Academies interpreted the Talmud, and expanded on the eras that were not clarified in the Babylonian Talmud. In *Megillah* tractate (7b) of the *Babylonian Talmud*, the following is written regarding the Purim:

> Rava said: A person is obligated to become intoxicated with wine on Purim until he is so intoxicated that he does not know how to distinguish between 'cursed is Haman' and 'blessed is Mordecai.'

The Rava in question is accepted as being Abba ben Joseph bar Hama, a Babylonian rabbi who lived between 280 and 352 AD. There is no parallel verse in the older Jerusalem Talmud, indicating the practice had been dropped in Judea / Palestine by 200 AD. The Jewish calendar is a lunisolar calendar, and so the 13th of Adar could fall anywhere in March on the Gregorian calendar.

According to various ancient sources, including Josephus and *Arabic Maccabees*, there was an engraved vineyard made from gold in the second temple, which Pompey took back to Rome after looting the temple in 63 BC. Josephus reported seeing the golden vineyard at the Temple of Zeus Capitolinus in Rome, and that it was inscribed with the words "The gift of Alexander, the king of Judea." This is accepted as King Alexander Jannaeus of Judea, who ruled between 103 and 76 BC, as he was the only Judean king named Alexander.

However, as Sabaoth was a god of wine, this suggests elements of Sabaoth worship continued under the Hasmonean kings. The latest surviving Roman references to Bacchus as the god in Judea are dated to 55 BC, after the civil war between Aristobulus II and Hyrcanus II over the kingship and high priesthood of Judea. Pompey had sided with Hyrcanus II and arrested Aristobulus II, who was sent to Rome in late 56 BC. Coins issued in Rome in 55 BC, celebrate the conquest of Syria and Judea by Pompey and include the name Bacchius Judaeus (BACCHIVS IVDAEUS) with a depiction of a man kneeling before an altar with a knife in one hand and a branch of some kind in the other. This is an odd depiction of a god and suggests that whichever god(s) the Judeans were worshiping, they were not carving traditional statues of them like the other nations.

The history of the Hasmonean kingdom is a history of civil wars between competing priesthoods, with Aristobulus and Hyrcanus' conflict simply being the most recent. This was a continuation of the conflicts between priesthoods described in the books of Ezra, set in the Persian era, and the Book of Kings (Septuagint's 3rd and 4th Kingdoms) set in the old kingdoms of Israel and Judea. In the earlier conflict, the different priesthoods represented different gods, and this may have been the situation in Hasmonean Judea as well.

The bulk of the religious fighting recorded in Judea during the Hasmonean dynasty was between the Sadducees and Pharisees, two competing priesthoods that interpreted the Judaic religion quite differently. The Sadducees appear to have had no problems with the syncretization of the Judean God with similar gods in other nations as long as the Torah was the supreme authority, not some other book. The Pharisees rejected this, and focused on the various ancient Canaanite and Aramaic texts written by Israelites and Judahites, rejecting all foreign influences. This indicates the Sadducees were the faction that accepted Sabaoth during the early Hasmonean era. They are recorded as being defeated and disarmed during the reign of Hyrcanus II, as they supported Aristobulus. Later, after Hyrcanus died and his widow Queen Salome Alexandra reigned, they fled Jerusalem as the Pharisees, who had not been disarmed were killing them. According to *Arabic Maccabees*, they settled with the Hasidians in the villages, suggesting the Hasidians had likewise lost power at some point, or conversely, never had any political power in the Hasmonean kingdom of Judea.

Strangely, in *Hebrew Maccabees*, neither the Sadducees nor Pharisees are mentioned, only the Hasideans, who are reported as supporting Judas' rebellion, but were not present at all of his battles. This is a clear indicator that he was leading another faction, which was likely the Sadducees, as there is no evidence of the Pharisees appearing until after the era of Simeon the Zealot. As *Hebrew Maccabees* was clearly a Hasidian text, and doesn't report any problems for the Hasidians under Judas rule, and no text indicates they ever had any political power within the Hasmonean dynasty, they may have simply remained out of politics after their right to worship was restored during Judas' wars.

Under Greek rule, the Judean God had been syncretized with the Phrgian god Sabazios, the Greek god Dionysis, the Roman god Bachhus, and the older Latin wine god Liber Pater. Sabazios was the god of the sky who rode a horse, was said to create earthquakes, and was represented by a 'hand.' Some have theorized that the god was partially based on descriptions of the Israelite god, as some Judeans were resettled in Phrygia during the Persian era. However, the Israelite God was described as riding on a 'cherub,' not a horse, and the iconography of the horse-god long predates the Judean settlement in the region. The Thracians, Trojans, and Bronze Age Greeks all worshiped a god that rode a flying horse, and was said to create earthquakes. The appointment of Philip the Phrygian as the High Preist in Jerusalem confirms that the two religions were seen as the same by many at the time.

Both Josephus and *Arabic Maccabees* confirm that the vineyard iconography continued to be used in the temple until shortly before the Herodian era, suggesting that Sabaoth the wine god did not disappear quickly, regardless of the redactions to the ancient scriptures that the Hasmonean dynasty made. This particular book strangely refers to Judas the Hammer as the 'Anointed of Sabaoth' many times, a term otherwise missing from ancient literature. Likewise, it refers to the Hasidians many times, a sect that is rarely mentioned in the other books. The reference to the 13th of Adar links a lost festival of the Anointed of Sabaoth with Purim, a festival originally dedicated to the god 'King', before the name 'King' was removed from the Hebrew translation of Esther.

In *Hebrew Maccabees*, Judas father Mattathias referred to his god by the title 'King,' which is the name or title the Hasidians called their god. This could be dismissed as a coincidence if this book didn't mention the Hasidians more than any other ancient book. The Hasidians were a sect of Judeans that were mentioned in several ancient sources, but died out or changed their name before the time of Josephus, and so little is known of them. In the Septuagint's *1ˢᵗ Maccabees*, the Asidaeoe (Ἀσιδαῖοι) were a sect of Judeans who supported Judas' rebellion. In *2ⁿᵈ Maccabees*, the author claims that Judas was a Hasidian, although this is not supported in other records, including this book. The Vetus Latina book of *Esther* also claims to be the 'Book of Hadassah, which is called Esther,' indicating it was a holy book of the Hasidian sect.

The nature of the sect is debated by scholars, some viewing them as a precursor to the Pharisees, and others viewing them as either a precursor or alternate name of the Essenes (Ἐσσηνοί) sect, who were mentioned by Josephus and others at the time. The Hebrew word chasidim (חֲסִידִים) translates as the plural form of pious (the 'pious' people), while the Greek name Essenes (Ἐσσηνοί) was defined by Philo of Alexandria circa 40 AD as meaning something like the plural form of 'holy' (the 'holy' people), which does support the connection between the groups. As the Essenes also followed the priesthood of Zedok (צדק), descended from the Solomonic priesthood, they are probably the source of the earliest Christian communities in Judea and Galilee, as the author of the *Letter to the Hebrews* made it clear that the church in Jerusalem was following the priesthood of Melchizedek, meaning 'King Ṣdq' (מלכי־צדק). Ṣdq, also translated as Zedok, Zedek, or Sydyk, was the Canaanite god of justice, similar to the Latin Jupiter.

The Vetus Latina book of *Esther* is significantly closer to both versions of *Esther* found in Septuagint manuscripts than to the abridged version found in the Masoretic texts, suggesting that the Hasidians influenced the development of the Septuagint and Vetus Latina manuscripts. The Masoretic version of Esther has had all references to God removed, indicating that the original text was considered heretical by the Pharisees. The Greek and Old Latin versions refer to God by the name or title 'King,' which would translated back to Hebrew as Mlk (מלך), the same spelling as the name of the god Moloch (מלך), whose worship had been purged under King Josiah circa 625 BC. Moloch is spelled as Mwlk (מולך) in modern literature to distinguish the name from the word for king, however, was spelled the same way as 'king' in the Masoretic texts. He is identified in the Masoretic book of *Kings* (Septuagint's *3ʳᵈ Kingdoms*) as being Ammonite and generally accepted as the archeo-logically attested Ammonite god Milkom (𐤌𐤋𐤊𐤌). Mlkm (𒀭𒈗) was also mentioned as a god in the Ugaritic texts from the 1300s BC, indicating that he had been worshiped in Canaan since the Bronze Age.

The Akkadian Cuneiform version of the word mlk (𐤌𐤋𐤊) was malkum (𒈠𒀠𒆳), meaning 'prince,' a title given to Nergal, the prince of the great city (under-world), and son of Ellil (𒀭𒂗𒇸), which also gave him the title of aplu ^{ilu}Ellil (𒌉 𒀭𒂗𒇸), meaning 'son of ^{god}Enlil.' In the Old Akkadian flood narrative of Atra-Hasis, Ellil was the god who caused the great flood, and his rival god Ia warned Atra-Hasis that the flood was coming, giving him enough time to build a huge box to shelter in with his family. After this flood, Atra-Hasis emerged from the box, which had floated down the river, and gave thanks to Ellil, Ia, and their father Ilu (god) for sparing his life.

In Syria, the name aplu ^{ilu}Ellil (𒌉 𒀭𒂗𒇸) was shortened to Aplu (𒌉) by the Hurrians, and adopted as Apaliunas (𒀊𒉺𒇷𒌋𒈾𒀸) by the Neshites (Hittites). Based on archeological evidence, Apaliunas was also worshipped by the Trojans, meaning that he was the 'Apollo' the Greeks recorded the Trojans worshipping during the Late Bronze Age. Earlier, during the Middle Bronze Age, the Amorites had called Resheph the 'son of

Ellil,' however, after the Hyksos dynasty fell the Amorite gods were initially suppressed, resulting in Resheph being called Shed (⁀⌐𓏛) in the Egyptian controlled parts of Canaan, which translates as 'savior,' as Resheph was believed to spare people from going to the Great City (underworld).

In the 20th century, the prominent biblical scholar William F. Albright proposed that the Canaanite god Melqart (𐤕𐤓𐤐𐤋𐤊) was also a version of this 'Prince of the Underworld,' as his name is generally accepted as originally being Mlk Qrt (𐤕𐤓𐤐 𐤊𐤋𐤌), meaning 'King of the City.' The city in question is usually assumed to be Tyre, however, he was widely worshiped throughout Phoenician colonies, including the colonies of Sidon and Byblos, which were the chief rivals of Tyre. If the 'city' was a reference to the underworld, as it was referred to in Babylonian literature, then Melqart, Milcom, and Moloch would be regional variants of the same Canaanite god of the underworld that Josiah banned the worship of circa 625 BC. As Melqart continued to be worshiped in Carthage and its colonies, there is no reason the banned Ammonite god Moloch would not have been.

In this book, Mattathias also called his god 'the king,' however, he later anoints his son Judas in the name of Sabaoth, suggesting he was practicing a form of Judaic polytheism that survived since the time before Josiah's reforms. As the Solomonic priesthood of Sydyk continued to operate in Judea, and was the priesthood of the Hasidians, and the Solomonic tradition was polytheistic, it suggests that Mattathias was a Hasidian priest. As the Vetus Latina version of the book of Esther, which includes the name 'King,' refers to itself as the 'Book of Hadassah, which is called Esther,' this indicates the Old Latin translation was made before the Hasmonean redactors removed all references to God from *Esther*.

The origin of the Purim festival is linked exclusively with the *Book of Esther*, and no other ancient Israelite or Judean text. It was mandated during the Persian era and therefore was practiced throughout the many lands that Persia ruled, so no Hasmonean redactors could have stopped the festival, however, the god 'King' was removed. As no known Jewish group has ever accepted *Hebrew Maccabees* as a religious text, and those associated with the text reported preserving it only for historical reasons, this suggests it is quite old, possibly dating back to the Second Temple Era, when there were still Hasidians around.

There are no other references to the Hasidian sect continuing to exist after the Maccabean Revolt, and *1*st *Maccabees* describes them being killed on the Sabbath as they refused to fight when attacked. There was a German Jewish sect that used the name 'Hasidian' in the

1300s, however, they are generally not accepted as being descended from the Classical era Hasidians. The gap between the Judean Hasidians and German Hasidians is over a thousand years, making the word 'Hasidian' in the text anomalous.

In the other books of the Maccabees, the word 'Hasidian' is generally only used once or twice. This seems to have been because the Greek and Arabic translators did not understand who the Hasidians were. They were not mentioned as partaking in the Sadducee-Pharisee war, however, in *Arabic Maccabees*, after the Sadducees lost power, they left Jerusalem and went to live with the Hasidians in the villages. This was described as happening during the reign of Queen Salome Alexandra, who reigned between 76 and 67 BC, indicating that the Hasidians were still active in Judea, but had no political power. *Arabic Maccabees* is not a reliable source, however, may nevertheless be correct in this, as there are no contradicting records.

Arabic Maccabees is a composite of various older Maccabean stories compiled in Palestinian Aramaic circa 525 AD and later translated into Arabic. Unfortunately, the author had little interest in historical accuracy, as the book appears to have been intended for adolescents. The first third of *Arabic Maccabees* is a reworking of *Hebrew Maccabees*, including the otherwise anomalous chapter

12, dealing with the life and death of Hannibal. The one and only manuscript that *Hebrew Maccabees* is found in, does not include any chapter structure, and so the chapter structure of *Arabic Maccabees* is imported. *Hebrew Maccabees* includes an introductory section that is not found in *Arabic Maccabees*, which is treated as a separate chapter in this translation, meaning the parallel content is found in chapters 2 through 18, which are chapters 1 through 17 in *Arabic Maccabees*.

Chapters 1 and 13 were likely additions made by the Hebrew translator, as they differ significantly from the rest of the book, and include a reference to the Talmud. The language of the book is a very pure form of Canaanite compared to the Aramaic-influenced form of Hebrew used in Judea. This suggests the Hebrew translation was made in Iberia, as the Samaritans and Judahites that fled the expanding Neo-Assyrian and Neo-Babylonian Empires, settled in the Carthaginian controlled regions of the western Mediterranean. These Iberian Israelites were never under the rule of the Assyrians, Babylonians, or Persians, all of whom used Aramaic as the official language in Canaan. Conversely, Carthage used the Punic form of Canaanite as an official language, and therefore, the form of Canaanite spoken by the Iberian Israelites remained purer than the form that developed into Hebrew in Judea.

Nevertheless, the book does contain several proper names that are spelled in Aramaic instead of Hebrew or Punic, supporting the majority of the book originating in the Aramaic language of Judea. There is also what appears to be a Punic word in chapter 4, suggesting this chapter was partially based on an older Punic book. The word is Tryygy (תרייגי), which is referred to as the place where the Phrygians and Romans came from. In the 1800s, it was interpreted as 'Trojans' based on context, however, this is unlikely as the Hebrew spelling of Trojans is Trwånm (טרויאנים). The word appears to be a transliteration of the Punic name for Thrace: Tryygy (𐤆𐤍𐤆𐤆𐤏𐤕).

Most modern forms of 'Thrace' are derived from the Greek Thracê (Θράκη), including the modern Hebrew Tråkyh (תראקיה). Conversely, the Punic form of the name was adopted earlier, and independent from Greek influence, as the Phoenicians had trading colonies in Thrace by 800 BC. Due to the close trade connections between the Carthaginians and Celtiberians, the Punic name was adopted into Celtic languages, and survived as late as the 700s AD in the Old Celtic form of the name: Traigia (𒑲 𒑺 𒑰 𒑺 𒑰). This was updated to the Greek-influenced Tráicia after the Latin alphabet became dominant. While the Romans are not accepted today as being descended from Thracians, the Phrygians are believed to have been an offshoot of the Thracians, based on linguistic analysis, and similar religious beliefs.

Chapter 4 also includes a strange reference to Philip the Phrygian as Philip Pelusium (פיליפוס הפלוסיום). Philip is not otherwise identified as coming from Pelusium, a city in eastern Egypt. This was likely an honorific title because he fought at the battle of Pelusium in 173 BC when Antiochus IV Epiphanes defeated the armies of Ptolemy VI Philometor. After he withdrew from the rest of Egypt, Pelusium remained a Seleucid-controlled city within Ptolemy's Egypt.

The names of countries that Hannibal conquered in chapter 13 date the Hebrew translation to sometime after 418 AD, as eastern Iberia is described as the Kingdom of the Goths (גותוס), and western Iberia is called 'Germania by the Sea of Oceanus.' Between 300 and 375, the Gothic Empire dominated the Germanic tribes north of the Roman Empire. Around 375, the Huns invaded the Gothic Empire from the east, and the Goths fled south of the Danube River seeking the protection of the Byzantine legions. Although Constantinople allowed the refugees to enter Byzantine territory, they didn't provide any food or shelter, and the Goths quickly turned on the Byzantines, initiating the Gothic War of 376 to 382. The Gothic War was followed by a civil war, in which Gothic units fought on both sides. In the early

400s, the Gothic legions united to occupy Italy, and in 418, established the Kingdom of the Goths, also called the Visigoths by the Byzantines, which dominated eastern Iberia (Spain) and southern Gaul (France).

In the text of chapter 13, western Iberia is called 'Germania by the Sea of Oceanus.' Between 300 and 375, the Gothic Empire dominated the Germanic tribes north of the Roman Empire. Around 375, the Huns invaded the Gothic Empire from the east, and the Goths fled south of the Danube River seeking the protection of the Byzantine legions. Although Constantinople allowed the refugees to enter Byzantine territory, they didn't provide any food or shelter, and the Goths quickly turned on the Byzantines, initiating the Gothic War of 376 to 382. The Gothic War was followed by a civil war, in which Gothic units fought on both sides. In the early 400s, the Gothic legions united to occupy Italy, and in 418, established the Kingdom of the Goths, also called the Visigoths by the Byzantines, which dominated eastern Iberia (Spain) and southern Gaul (France).

Like chapter 1, chapter 13 is not historically accurate, however, the rest of the book appears to be accurate in comparison to other sources, such as Josephus, with the exception of the ongoing references to the Hasidians and the Anointed of Sabaoth. Comparing the Hannibal chapters (13 in this book, and 12 in *Arabic Maccabees*), they both contain many of the same errors, however, the Hebrew version is more historically accurate. Both Hannibal chapters refer to Hannibal as the king of Africa, which is not accurate, as he was a statesman and general, but not a king. Africa was the Latin name of modern Tunisia, based on the word ifri (ΣΗΟΣ), Amazigh (Berber) for 'cave,' as most of the indigenous settlements in the region were built underground. The Romans saw the Carthaginians as foreign invaders who had conquered and enslaved the Ifri, and were trying to do the same thing to the Iberians, Scilians, Sardinians, and Corsicans. The 1st Punic War began when the Carthaginians started to do this to the Italians, and the tiny republic of Rome decided they would not be subject to Carthage.

The term 'Africa' was not applied to the entire continent until a few hundred years ago, and so the Africa in the text would have been a reference to the Roman province. 'Africa' was the name of the province from 146 BC until 439 AD, and again between 534 and 698. Between 439 and 534 it was known as the Vandal Kingdom, as the Germanic Vandal tribe had occupied the region as the western half of the Byzantine Empire collapsed. As the author used the name 'Goths,' he would have probably also used the name 'Vandals,' and so the translation likely took place between 418 and 439. The author of Arabic Maccabees used it as a source around 525, which means it could not have been translated after the kingdom of the Vandals fell to Byzantium in 534.

Both versions of the Hannibal chapter include many other errors, proving they have a common origin. In both chapters, Hannibal flees to Egypt after his defeat but is sent back to Carthage, where he takes his own life. In fact, Hannibal was defeated in battle and then spoke in the Carthaginian Senate in favor of the terms the Romans had imposed on Carthage. In both chapters, Hannibal's brother Hasdrubal is killed by General Scipio, who then cuts off Hasdrubal's head and sends it to Hannibal. This is a confused abridgment of what actually happened.

Hannibal did have a brother known as Hasdrubal ben Barca (𐤁𐤓𐤒 𐤁𐤍 𐤏𐤆𐤓𐤁𐤏𐤋), however, he died five years before Scipio's invasion of Africa. The initial defense of Carthage was led by Hasdrubal ben Gisco (𐤁𐤍 𐤏𐤆𐤓𐤁𐤏𐤋 𐤂𐤓𐤔𐤊𐤍), who committed suicide shortly after Scipio defeated him. Hannibal and his other brother Mago (𐤌𐤂𐤍) returned from Italy with their armies to defend Carthage. Historians debate what happened to Mago, with most accepting the Roman historian Livy's account, recorded in the 1st century AD, that Mago died at sea before reaching Africa. Conversely, the earlier Roman historian Cornelius Nepos, writing in the 1st century BC, reported that he fought in Africa, and later traveled with Hannibal until the Carthaginian senate arrested him in 193 BC. Nepos reported that after he escaped custody he later died in a shipwreck. Hannibal's brother Hasdrubal's head was cut off, however, it was five years before Scipio's invasion of Africa, by Claudius Nero after the battle of Metaurus, in Italy. Nero had it packed in a sack and thrown into Hannibal's camp, similar to what Scipio did in both Hannibal chapters.

Regardless of the similarities, there are also differences that show the Hebrew chapter on Hannibal to be older than the Arabic, however, the Arabic retains some different details. The Hebrew chapter includes the names of Italian locations where major battles were fought that are missing from the Arabic chapter. The Arabic chapter mentions battles in Italy but does not name the locations of the battles. The Hebrew chapter claims he sailed to the town Qnwsi (קנוסי), on the Ååwpydws (אאופידוס) river, and then fought a battle against Aemilius and Varro where 90,000 Roman soldiers died. This is a description of the Battle of Cannae on the Aufidus River, which is today called the Ofanto River.

The Arabic chapter then deviates, mentioning that Varro withdrew to a fortified city called Venusia, which did happen, but it is not mentioned in the Hebrew chapter. This can only have been derived from another historical text consulted by the author of *Arabic Maccabees*. The Hebrew chapter skips past Venusia and has the Romans regrouping at a town called Knwsyah (כנוסיאה). After his initial retreat to Venusia, Varro heard that a larger group of Roman soldiers was regrouping in Canusium, and traveled there to take command. As none of the Hebrew names were incorporated into the Arabic chapter, it is likely the author of *Arabic Maccabees* was not sure which towns were being referenced, and so looked up the names in a Latin or Greek book about Hannibal, where she found the name Venusia. *Arabic Maccabees* is written from a somewhat feminist perspective, and the author likely included the name as the town is named after a goddess.

Arabic Maccabees also deviates significantly from *Hebrew Maccabees* theologically, and never once calls God 'the King,' or calls Judas the 'Anointed of Sabaoth.' The author of *Arabic Maccabees* was focused on writing a 'mythic-tale,' that was not intended to be treated as real history. She referred to Judea as the 'Holy Land,' and Jerusalem as the 'City of the Sacred Temple,' evoking the imagery of a long-lost time and place.

The author did mention the Hasidians in passing, however, the Arabic translator did not understand the reference, and wrote the following about them, likely earlier than 1200 AD based on the Arabic dialect:

The author of this book did not describe their rules, nor do we know anything of them other than their name, as they applied themselves to practices that were more the eminent virtues, namely, to select from those two other sects whichever was most safe in belief, most sure and guarded.

The description provided is essentially what the German Hasidians of the 1300s and the modern Hassidic Jews do, erring on the side of caution in the implementation of their laws and customs. The strange religious terminology is unique to *Hebrew Maccabees*, and other than chapters 1 and 13, appears to date to an older era, or undocumented Judaic cult that continued the practice of the Hellenistic Judeans. As a result, most modern scholars are leery of delving into the book, and instead focus on the collection the book is found in. The collection was bought by the Bodleian Library in Oxford from Rabbi Rabbinowitz in 1887, however, its earlier history is a matter of debate. Rabbinowitz claimed to have previously bought it in Italy, however, that is as far back as its ownership can be traced.

The collection was named the *Hebrew Bible Historiale* by the Royal Asiatic Society, who hired Moses Gaster to translate it in 1899. The collection of texts was comprised of various legendary 'historical' stories drawn from other known sources, a story about the persecution of the Jews during the Crusades, various poems and astrological observations, and a collection of stories in a pure form of Hebrew. The larger collection of stories and poems, the *Hebrew Bible Historiale*, was collected by Eleasar ben Asher the Levite, who lived in Germany in the early 1300s. Eleasar left a preface to the work, in which he claimed to have collected the books and short stories from many diverse sources, and asked his descendants to preserve it, as it was his life's work. It is assumed that the occasional Yiddish word or comment in the collection is his work.

The subset of stories within the *Hebrew Bible Historiale* written in the pure form of Hebrew is identified as being a collection that Jerahmeel ben Solomon compiled in southern Italy in the 1200s. Gaster dubbed this collection the *Chronicles of Jerahmeel* to differentiate it from the larger collection Eleasar had compiled. This collection of texts itself is unusual, as the texts are not woven into a consistent narrative like the Hebrew versions of *Josippon* (ספר יוסיפון) and *Jashur* (ספר הישר), both of which are also generally accepted as being composed in Southern Italy, *Josippon* in the 10th century, and *Jashur* in the 16th century. Gaster strongly disputed the dating of both these texts as being artificially younger, as the analysis was based on faulty later Latin translations. Gaster believed that both of these works were reworked from much older sources, likely originally translated in Iberia, based on the pure form of Hebrew used, which is not otherwise documented in Italy. Gaster included the *Chronicles of Jerahmeel* as part of this older vein of pure Hebrew literature.

Within the *Chronicles of Jerahmeel*, all the books are set before *Hebrew Maccabees*, or, as Jarahmeel called it, the 'Book of the Maccabee.' The term 'maccabee' (מכבי) is somewhat debated, as Jews generally interpret it as an acronym for the Torah expression, "Mi chamocha ba'elim Yhwh!" found in Exodus. This translates as "Which of the Lords is like you, Yahweh?" This analysis is generally rejected by academics, as the name Yahweh was not in the book of Exodus used in the time of Judas. It was reintroduced by Judas' younger brother Simon the Zealot after he became high priest and king of Judea. According to Masoretic Divrei-hayyamim (Septuagint's 2nd Paralipomenon), the Sanhedrin tractate (104a) in the Talmud, and the Seder Olam, the 'name of God' had been removed from the Torah during the reign of King Manasseh in the 7th century BC.

The Hasmoneans 'restored' the name when they produced the Hebrew translation, and ordered all the older Aramaic, Judahite, and Samaritan copies in circulation to be destroyed. The Judeans in Judea and the rest of the Middle East were speaking Aramaic at the time, which resulted in the creation of the Targums, Aramaic language translations of the Torah. The interpretation of 'Maccabee' generally accepted by academics, is that it was the Aramaic word mkkbå (מקּבָא), meaning 'hammer.' Based on this interpretation of the word, the original name of the *Hebrew Maccabees* would have been the *Book of the Hammer*.

Other than the strange religious terminology, the bulk of the content of chapters 2 through 12 and 14 through 18 is found in other ancient sources, including Septuagint's *1ˢᵗ* and *2ⁿᵈ Maccabees,* and Josephus' *Antiquities of the Judeans*, all in Greek, and the Hebrew language *Josippon* and *Jashur*. The Latin *Josippon* deviates significantly from the Hebrew, and the English *Jashur* is an unrelated book generally regarded as an 18ᵗʰ century forgery by Jacob Ilive. *Chronicles of Jerahmeel* is closest to *Josippon* and *Jashur*, which has led some scholars to propose it was based on *Josippon*, as *Jashur* is generally dated to later. However, Gaster concluded the opposite, as both *Josippon* and *Jashur* merge the books into an ongoing narrative, which Jerahmeel did not do. In the *Chronicles of Jerahmeel*, each book and short story stands alone, copied in the original form, as Jerahmeel found it.

Hebrew Maccabees is also quite different from the versions of the Maccabean histories found in *Josephus*,

Josippon, and *Jashur*, as it ends with the death of Judas the Hammer, the Anointed of Sabaoth. It reads as if it was written shortly after he died, before the religious reforms of Simon the Zealot. According to Roman records the Judean god changed abruptly from Bacchus (Dionysus, Sabaoth, Pater Liber) to Jupiter-Sabazius between 142 and 139 BC, and suddenly included astrology. This was recorded by Valerius Maximus:

> Gnaeus Cornelius Hispalus, praetor peregrinus in the year of the consulate of Marcus Popilius Laenas and Lucius Calpurnius, ordered the astrologers by an edict to leave Rome and Italy within ten days, since by a fallacious inter-pretation of the stars they perturbed fickle and silly minds, thereby making profit out of their lies. The same praetor compelled the Jews, who attempted to infect the Roman custom with the cult of Jupiter Sabazius, to return to their home.

This 'Jupiter Sabazius' (IOVIS SABAZIUS) is no doubt the Yhwh ṣbåwt (צבאות יהוה) of the Hebrew scriptures the Hasmoneans produced. Yhwh and Jupiter were commonly pronounced quite similarly, as Jova and Jovis, which could have confused the Romans. The Hasmonean dynasty later prohibited the pronunciation of the name, after the extreme response their closest ally had. The Masoretic version of the Torah's chronology is also deeply corrupted by astrology compared to the older Septuagint translation. It is not clear if the astrology was

29

already in the Judahite texts the Hasmoneans translated, or if they introduced it. A simple example of this is the Exodus of the Israelites from Egypt, which in the Septuagint takes place within 3 years of the estimated date of the Minoan eruption according to Egyptologists. Josephus also correlated the Exodus with the fall of the Hyksos Dynasty, which happened three years after the Minoan eruption according to Egyptologists. In the Masoretic version, it happened hundreds of years later, at a well-documented era in Egyptian history, when nothing vaguely similar was recorded.

This corruption is rooted in the interpretation of the creation of the world happening in 3760 BC, which happens to be when the constellation Taurus became the marker of the Northern Winter Solstice. Taurus was the asterism that the ancient Canaanites called El (✳, ≣Ⲓ, ∠✦), meaning 'god,' and began the age of El (god). This idea was adopted along with the Babylonian calendar during the Babylonian captivity, and so may have been the Judahite language version of the Torah used in Jerusalem before the Hasmonean dynasty, but probably wasn't. Modifications made to a Judahite language copy of the Torah are unlikely under Babylonian or Persian rule, as the Aramaic version of the Torah was in common use, and based on the Septuagint's translation, could not have been altered by the astrologers. The most likely time for the alterations to have been made was when the Hasmonean dynasty changed the common language of the Torah from Aramaic to Hebrew. This would also explain why Judeans were suddenly grouped together with the astrologers in 139 BC, during the reign of High Priest and King Simon the Zealot.

Some scholars have suggested the translation was made under the rule of Judas and Simon's brother Jonathan, who was the high priest between 161 and 143 BC, after Judas, but before Jonathan. This is based on his nickname, which is variously listed as Apphous (Απφους), Sapphous (Σαπφους), Saphphous (Σαφφους), Apphous (Απφους), and Samphous (Σαμφους) in Septuagint manuscripts. This is theorized by some scholars to be based on the Aramaic word hoppws (הׄיׄפׄפׄוׄס), meaning 'disassembler' or 'transliterator.' The meaning of the nickname is debated, and it is sometimes interpreted as a Greek transliteration of the Aramaic word åpws (אׄיׄפׄוׄס), which is itself both adopted from the Greek epos (έπος), meaning 'poet,' and the old Canaanite åps (𐤏𐤐𐤎), meaning 'extreme,' although by the Classical era interpreted as åpws (אׄפׄוׄס), meaning 'annihilate.' This means that Jonathan's nickname could have been the 'transliterator,' 'poet,' or 'annihilator.'

Unfortunately, this book does not shed light on Jonathan's role, as the book ends when Judas the

31

Hammer dies, just before Jonathan became High Priest. Regardless of whether it was Jonathan or Simon, someone produced a Hebrew translation of the Torah during their rule, as some of the Hebrew language Torah fragments among the Dead Sea Scrolls date back to the beginning of Simon's reign. Simon is also the king who insisted everyone update their Torah, and appointed government-funded scribes to update the Torah for whoever brought in an older copy. His government also mandated that all old copies of the Torah be burned so they would not mislead people.

The reforms under the Hasmoneans radically altered the concept of Sabaoth, which was no longer the name of God, but an epithet meaning 'forces.' The repeated references to Judas as the 'Anointed of Sabaoth' suggest chapters 8 through 18, other than chapter 13 on Hannibal, were written before the reforms, as a book about the Anointed of Sabaoth. Chapter 7 was likely part of this *Book of the Anointed of Sabaoth*, as it is the chapter that includes Mattathias' referring to his god as 'King,' however, is mostly about Judas' actions while his father was the high priest. Chapter 7 also includes what appears to be a scribal note mentioning the *Book of Joseph ben Gurion*, which would have been written in the late 1st century AD, in Greek and/or Aramaic, and likely served as the basis of the *Josippon*.

The references to the Hasidians are found throughout the chapters that appear to have originated in the Book of the Anointed of Sabaoth, as well as chapter 4, which also includes the obscure reference to Philip the Phrygian as Philip Pelusium. However, chapter 4 also includes the Punic name of Thrace, indicating it started as a Punic text, not Aramaic like the Book of the Anointed of Sabaoth. As both the Aramaic and Punic books appear to have been Hassidian texts, it is likely that they were preserved in Iberia by Hassidians during the reforms in Judea, like the Old Latin version of Esther was preserved in Italy.

Chapter 1 is a compilation of Rabbinical history of the Persian era, and references the Talmud, indicating it was likely written after 400 AD. Based on content, chapters 2, 3, and 5 may be derived from Jason of Cyrene's now lost 5-volume *History of the Maccabees*. The content is mirrored in the Septuagint's *1st* and *2nd Maccabees*, and the author of *2nd Maccabees* wrote a long preface in which he claimed to be abridging Jason's longer work. The purity of the language suggests these chapters were not based on the Greek translations, however, that is also a possibility. The Hebrew *Josippon* is also a possible source for these stories, however, the style of *Josippon* suggests it was compiled after *Hebrew Maccabees*. Chapter 13 on Hannibal was likely derived from an

Iberian story about Hannibal, as it is otherwise missing from the pure Hebrew language histories that Gaster identified.

The anonymous author of the *Josippon* claimed to be copying the ancient writings of Joseph ben Gorion (יוסף בן גוריון), which is generally assumed to be a reference to Josephus, however, Josephus' father's name was Matthias. The association of these two men named Joseph/Josephus first appeared in the scribal notes in a copy of the Latin language *On the Destruction of Jerusalem*. The 4th century book itself identifies a prefect in Jerusalem as Josephum Gorione Genitum, which the scribe claimed in the notes was Josephus. While the connection with Josephus is generally ignored by historians, *On the Destruction of Jerusalem* does support the existence of Joseph ben Gorion in Jerusalem during the same era as Josephus. The Josippon is a chronicle of Jewish history from Adam to the 1st century AD, ending during the reign of Emperor Titus who ruled Rome between 79 and 81 AD. This suggests it was originally written during his rule.

The *Josippon* became very popular in Western Europe after the invention of the printing press, which has led to a great deal of scholarly debate about its origin. European scholars have pulled the work apart and come to many conflicting views about its origin, however, generally agree it is a composite work, originally compiled in Hebrew in southern Italy in the 10th century, based on older Greek and Latin works, like the writings of Josephus and *On the Destruction of Jerusalem*. This original Josippon was then expanded by Judah Leon ben Moses Mosconi in the 1300s before being printed in 1476.

While the expansion by Mosconi is not debated, the origin of the Hebrew work is, as the Andalusian historian Abū Muḥammad Alī ibn Aḥmad ibn Saīd ibn Ḥazm had an Arabic translation of it, which he obtained from a Yemeni Jew. Ibn Ḥazm was a prolific writer, who produced over 400 books before his death in 1064 BC, and his account is not doubted, so some scholars have suggested an earlier date for the original Hebrew work, in the 9th century. The Arabic name of the book ibn Ḥazm referred to, was called Ywsybws (يوسـيبوس), which is an Arabic transliteration of the Greek spelling of Josephus: Iôsêpos (Ἰώσηπος). This makes it unlikely that the Arabic translation was made from the Hebrew *Josippon*, which claims to be a copy of the writing of 'Joseph ben Gorion,' which transliterates more directly as Ywsp bn Gwrywn (יוסף בן גוריון).

The most likely origin of the divergent Hebrew, Latin, and Arabic versions of *Josippon* is Joseph ben Gorion originally publishing two versions, as he was literate in both Aramaic and Greek. It is unlikely he would have penned the Hebrew version directly, as virtually no one in Judea could read Hebrew. The Hebrew translation would have probably been made in Iberia for the Western Mediterranean Jews, while the Greek version would have been translated into Latin and Arabic.

In any event, *Hebrew Maccabees*, which includes a note that refers to the Book of Joseph ben Gorion, is clearly not his book. If the note is accepted as a scribal note by the translator, Chapter 7 could be interpreted as part of the original Book of the Anointed of Sabaoth, however, if the note is accepted as part of the original text, it places the origin of chapter 7 in the late 1st century AD at the earliest, instead of shortly after 160 BC. As chapter 7 includes the reference to the Hasidians and refers to God as 'King,' it is anachronistic in the late 1st century AD, and so it seems probable that the Hebrew translator added it in the 5th century, like the note regarding the Talmud in chapter 1.

Chapter 1

In the first year of his reign, Cyrus[1] tried to build the temple, but when Ahasuerus[2] arose he prohibited it and attempted to destroy the vineyard. God killed him and the evil Haman from the world, and he died. His son succeeded him. These are the kings mentioned: Darius, Cyrus, and Artaxerxes.[3] Then the people believed in the prophets and were prosperous. In the second year of his reign, he allowed the Judahites to return to Jerusalem to build the sacred temple and repair Jerusalem without limitation or hindrance. This was a complete redemption.

Then Ezra, Zerubbabel, and his company went for the second time to Jerusalem with another generation of the captives, and they rebuilt Jerusalem and its walls. The towers that they erected were very high and strong, and the temple contained more than the first one so the first temple was considered insignificant in comparison to it. Because of this, the people served Cyrus loyally for thirty-four years.[4]

After the rebuilding of the temple, Zerubbabel returned to Babylon and there died. His son, Meshullam, succeeded him, and in his days, in the fifty-second year of the kingdom of the Medes and Persians,[5] the kingdom was formed. The last prophets, Haggai, Zechariah, and Malachi,[6] died at that time, and from that day prophecy ceased to exist in Israel, and the Echo of the Heavenly

Voice took its place, and after that, they had to consult the rabbis, until the Messiah will come and show us the right way.

Thirty-four years after the rebuilding of the temple,[7] Darius, the son of Ahasuerus, reigned, until Alexander the Macedonian, and first King of Greece, rose up against him in battle, killed him, and captured his kingdom.[8] He reigned over Israel for two years and captured every kingdom. He made the whole world subservient to him. At that time, thirty-four years after the rebuilding of the temple, Alexander the Great was crowned, the son of Philippus, King of Macedon, for he made the name of the Macedonian nation great, and conquered the whole world.

When he waged war against Darius he attacked the land of Egypt and slaughtered in Alexandria twice as many Judeans as escaped from Egypt.[9] After conquering Edom, he marched along the seashore until he came to Acre,[10] which he conquered, as well as Ashkelon and Gaza.[11] He then turned to go up to Jerusalem to attack it, because the Judeans had made an alliance with Darius. After journeying with all his camp some distance, he arrived at a lodge, where he and his army camped.

That night as he was lying in his bed in his tent, he opened his eyes and saw a man standing over him, clothed in white linen, and with a drawn sword in his hand. The sword looked like lightning on a stormy day. He lifted the sword over the head of the king, and he was terrified, and said, "Why will my lord kill his servant?"

The man replied, "God has sent me to conquer kings and many nations before you, and I will go before you to render you assistance but know that you will now be killed because your heart is intent on going to Jerusalem to injure God's priests and God's people."

"I beg you, lord," replied the king, "pardon the sin of your servant, and if it is evil in your eyes, I will return to my home."

"Don't be afraid," the man said. "Go to Jerusalem, and when you approach the gate of the city and see a man clothed in white like me, having an appearance and form like mine, immediately bow before him and lay down on the ground before him. Do whatever he commands you and do not transgress his word, for the very day that you rebel against his word you will be killed."

The king woke and traveled to Jerusalem. When the High Priest heard that the king was coming against Jerusalem in great anger, he was terrified, as were all the people, and he went with the people out to the gate of the city, and he stood before them clothed in white linen. As soon as Alexander saw the priest, he quickly dismounted from his chariot, fell down on his face, and bowed down to him. The generals of Alexander became very angry at this, and demanded, "Why do you bow down to a man who has no strength for battle?"

The king replied, "Because the man that goes in front of me to subdue all the nations before me looks like this man. I therefore bow down to him."

Then, going into our holy temple, he said to the priest, "I will have my statue erected here and will give a great deal of gold to the workers, so it may be a memorial to me. They shall erect it between the Holy of Holies and the temple so that my image should be remembered in this great temple of God."

The priest replied, "Donate the gold for the maintenance of God's priests and the poor of His people, and I will make you remembered forever, as you want. All the children of the priests that are born this year will be called by your name, Alexander, and you will be remembered when they worship in this temple. However, it is not allowed to place an engraved image or any statue in the temple of our God."

The king then gave the gold according to the priest's request. He asked him to inquire of God on his behalf whether he should go to war with Darius, or abandon the plan. The priest replied, "He will certainly be given into your hands."

Then, he brought out the book of Daniel, and he showed him the passage concerning the ram that gores on all sides and the goat kid which runs up to him and tramples upon him. "You," he explained, "are the goat kid and Darius is the ram. You will therefore trample upon him and seize his kingdom."

After this, Alexander went to battle and killed Darius. He captured his entire kingdom so that the Persian kingdom ceased to exist. Alexandria in Egypt was made the royal city.

He ruled over all the nations just as a shepherd rules over his flock. He soon traveled to India, venturing right across the country to its farthest reaches, and extended his dominion, (as we learn from the Talmud. R. Jose said, "For six years he reigned in Elam, and afterward spread his kingdom over the whole world.")[12]

He reigned altogether for twelve years, and when he was on his way home to his house he died. Before his death, he divided his kingdom among his four generals. He made Ptolemy the son of Lagus[13] the king of Egypt, Philip his brother the king of Macedon, and Seleucus and Nicanor kings of Syria and Babylon respectively.[14]

CHAPTER 1

Finally, he appointed Antiochus, the great enemy of the Judeans as king of Asia.[15]

Daniel prophesied this event when he said that the goat would gore the ram and break down his kingdom, which would be given to the four winds of the sky.

Chapter 1 Notes

1 Hebrew: Kwrš (כורש)

This is the Hebrew spelling of the name of King Kūruš (𐎤𐎢𐎽𐎢𐏁), known today as Cyrus II, based on his Greek name Cyros ho Presbyteros (Κῦρος ὁ Πρεσβύτερος), meaning 'Cyrus the Elder.' King Cyrus of Persia and Media conquered Lydia and Babylon, creating the Persian Empire. He released the Judahite and other Canaanite peoples that Babylon had conquered to create a buffer zone between Egypt and his fledgling empire. His son Cambyses later annexed this buffer zone before invading and occupying Egypt and Cyrene.

2 Hebrew: Achashverosh (אֲחַשְׁוֵרוֹשׁ). Translation: Xerxes

Achashverosh, more commonly rendered as Ahasuerus, is the Hebrew name of Xšayār̥šā (𐎧𐏁𐎹𐎠𐎼𐏁𐎠), today known as King Xerxes I, who ruled between 486 and 465 BC, and was the father of Artaxerxes I. Xerxes is Old Iranian for 'ruling over heroes,' which was translated into Babylonian as Aḫšiyaršu (𒄴𒅆𒅀𒅈𒋗), and then transliterated into Hebrew as Achashverovosh (אֲחַשְׁוֵרוֹשׁ) in Masoretic Ezra-Nehemiah and Esther. The English name Xerxes is derived from the Greek transliteration Xerxês (Ξέρξης), however, both of the versions of Esther found in Septuagint manuscripts use a name other than Xerxes to translate Achashverosh. The common translation, found in the Codex Vaticanus, Codex Sinaticaus, Codex Alexandrius, and most other manuscripts uses the name Artaxerxes (Αρταξερξου), while the rarer and probably older Alpha texts version of Esther uses the name Assyeros (Ασσερος), which is a transliteration of the Hebrew name. Likewise, the Vetus Latina translators did not know for Xerxes was, and transliterated the name into Latin as Asuerus.

The 1st century AD Judean Historian Josephus also claimed that Artaxerxes (Ἀρταξέρξου) was the Greek translation of Åḥšwrwš (אחשורוש), a view repeated in Josippon in the 10th century, and the Esther Rabbah in the 11th century. This reference to Ahasuerus in the same sentence as Haman confirmes that the author has skipped to a different century, and is referring to the events in Esther, which are almost certainly set during the reign of Xerxes I (486 to 465 BC), however, the author then jumps back to Cyrus II (559 to 530 BC), releasing the Judahites from Babylon again for some reason, suggesting a second Persian king named Cyrus repeated the actions of the first. Cyrus II was the second and last Cyrus among the Achaemenid kings of the Persian Empire, the first being his grandfather Cyrus I, who was mentioned by the Judahite prophet Isaiah.

The confusion over what happened during the Persian Era is common in Judean texts, as most of what happened in Jerusalem was purged from the records by Ezra the scribe after evicting the various priesthoods that had been operating in Jerusalem. Josephus claimed to be given the records from the temple in Jerusalem when the Romans sacked it, and some have theorized that these records were later handed down in the form of the Josippon, the Book of Jashur, or the Chronicles of Jerahmeel. The core of the confusion over the Persian era appears to be caused by the fact that many Persian kings had only a few names, there were two kings named Cyrus, three named Darius, four named Artaxerxes, and two named Xerxes. The books of Ezra, Nehemiah, and Esther do not clarify which king is being referred to, resulting in the Rabbinical version of Persian history, in which there was one of Cyrus, on Darius, and one Ahasuerus, who ruled Persia for a few decades between the fall of Babylon and the rise of Macedonia.

3 Hebrew: Artachshaste (אַרְתַּחְשַׁסְתָּא). Translation: Artaxerxes

The reference to Artachshaste as a separate name from Achashverosh confirms that Achashverosh was originally a reference to Xerxes, not Artaxerxes.

4 Cyrus II was only king of Babylon for 9 years before he died. Including his earlier reign as king of Persia before the conquest of Babylon, his reign was 29 years. There is no evidence that Judah was under the rule of Persia during his reign. No Persian kings are recorded as ruling for exactly 34 years. Like the rest of Rabbinical chronology of the Persian era, this cannot be synchronized with the actual history of the era.

5 The unification of the kingdoms of Media and Persia took place in 550 BC according to Persian records. 52 years later was 498 BC, during the reign of Darius I. If the author was thinking of the era from the conquest of Babylon in 539 BC, then 52 years later would have been the first full year of Xerxes I's reign, the Ahasuerus from the book of Esther.

6 Both the prophets Haggai and Zechariah were active in the year 520 BC, although it is not clear when they died. Who and when Malachi was is debated.

7 Based on the books of Ezra, the temple was rebuilt by Ezra in 351 BC.

8 Alexander III of Macedon conquered the Persian Empire during the reign of Darius III, however, his father was named Arsames. The previous Persian king was Artaxerxes IV, who was poisoned by Bagoas, the person most directly responsible for the collapse of the Persian Empire. Bagoas was a Persian court eunuch who gained massive wealth during the Persian wars to suppress the rebellions in Canaan and Egypt by sacking the temples after the Persian armies had defeated the local militias and armies. He orchestrated the assassination of Artaxerxes III, the Artaxerxes from the era of Ezra, as well as Artaxerxes III's whole family other than his son Artaxerxes IV, whom he placed on the throne as a puppet. A few years later Artaxerxes IV attempted to have Bogoas killed, however, Bogoas learned of the plot and killed Artaxerxes IV, following which he placed Darius III on the throne. Due to Bagoas' interference, Artaxerxes IV and Darius III were unable to properly rule the empire, and as a result, the empire was already collapsing when Alexander III invaded.

9 Alexander III did not attack Egypt, he captured the Tyre and Gaza en route to Egypt and was welcomed in Egypt as a liberator. He offered sacrifices to the Egyptian gods, and visited the sanctuary of Amen in the Siwa oasis, where he was recognized as the son of Amen. He then founded Alexandria, a city he named after himself. The city was founded on a small peninsula, that would be easy to defend if the Egyptians revolted.

10 Hebrew: Akko (עַכּוֹ). Translation: Acre

The city of Acre (עַכּוֹ / ‏ﻋﻜ‎), in northern modern Israel, was known as Ôkå (𓂝𓄿𓈎𓏤) to the ancient Egyptians, while the Phoenician name was Ôk (𐤏𐤊). Before the conquest of Alexander III, the city was known as Aco (Ἄκο) or Acê (Ἄκη) in Greek. The Greeks renamed it Antiochia Ptolemaes (Ἀντιόχεια Πτολεμαΐς) and later simplified that to Ptolemaes (Πτολεμαΐς) during the Hellenic era. The Romans later renamed it Colonia Claudii Caesaris Ptolemais, and then shortened that to Colonia Ptolemais. Latin crusaders renamed the city Sainct-Jehan-d'Acre, which they then simplified to Acre. The use of the older name here, suggests the text was written in Iberia, where the Hebrew language was never influenced directly by Aramaic and Greek, and maintained its older form. The Judahites established colonies in Iberia and Northwest Africa when Carthage dominated the region, and unlike other Judahites in the Middle East, were never under the rule of Babylon or Persia, and never adopted Aramaic. After the Romans defeated the Carthaginians, the Judahites in Iberia appear to have transitioned seamlessly from Punic to Hasmonean Hebrew. Hebrew remained in use in Iberia among Jews throughout history, requiring the Jews in Babylon to translate their Aramaic letters into Hebrew before sending them to Iberia.

11 Hebrew: Azzah (עַזָּה). Translation: Gaza

Alexander is only recorded as fighting two major battles in Canaan, the Siege of Tyre, and the Siege of Gaza. The rest of Syria, Judea, and Egypt surrendered without any significant battles. Alexander was wounded at Gaza, and after conquering the city, executed all the men, and sold the woman and children as slaves, as he had previously done in Tyre.

12 The reference is from the Avodah Zarah tractate found in both the Jerusalem and Babylonian Talmuds (Folio 10a). The quote in the Talmud is from Rabbi Jose ben Halafta, who lived in the second century AD. The reference to the Talmud dates the line to sometime after the year 400, as the Talmud is generally dated to then.

13 Hebrew: Tlmy bn Lågi (לאגי תלמי בן). Translation: Ptolmey son of Lagus

Ptolemy I Soter (Πτολεμαῖος Σωτήρ) was the founder of the Ptolemaic dynasty of Egypt. His legal father was Lagus (Λάγος), a Macedonian courtier who married King Philip II of Macedon's former concubine Arsinoe. It was rumored that she was already pregnant with Ptolemy, which would make him Alexander III's illegitimate half-brother. Modern scholars generally dismiss the claim as later propaganda. In this verse, the author has decided to take a stand on this question for some reason, as he does not list the other kings' fathers.

14 Seleucus I Nicator (Σέλευκος Νικάτωρ) was a single person, who founded the Selucid Empire, adopting the title 'Lord of Asia.' His initial empire included the eastern half of the former Persian empire, spanning modern Iran and Iraq. He later conquered Syria, which had initially been under the control of Antigonus I Monophthalmus.

15 While Alexander III did reign for 12 years after conquering Persia, he did not divide his empire among the generals but left no heir. His wife Roxanna was pregnant at the time, and his brother Philip had a noticeable mental development issue. The generals then tore his empire apart, resulting in Ptolemy's kingdom of Egypt, Seleucid's empire in Asia, the Kingdom of Lysimachus in Anatolia and Thrace, and the Kingdom of Macedon. The first Antiochus, Antiochus

I Soter, was the son of Seleucus I Nicator, founder of the
Seleucid Empire.

Chapter 2

When Seleucus[1] reigned over Macedonia,[2] a very wicked, rebellious man of our own people, Simeon of the tribe of Benjamin, went to Seleucus and slandered the Judeans. He informed him of the riches contained in the temple at Jerusalem, saying that the treasures were heaped up in the treasury in endless quantities, and an abundance of gold and precious stones, and that it would be preferable to have it all placed in the treasury of Seleucus. The king therefore sent for Heliodorus, the captain of his army, and ordered him to go to Jerusalem with his armies. On his arrival, Onias[3] the priest asked him, "Why has my lord come to his servants?"

"Because of the vast amount of gold and precious stones which, the king has been told about, which is contained in the treasury of your temple," (he answered.)

"The only gold in the treasury," answered the priest, "is that which King Seleucus and other kings presented to us, for the maintenance of orphans, widows, and the poor. For this, we pray to God to grant long life to the king and his sons."

However, Heliodorus would not listen to the priest and placed soldiers around the temple until the following day, when the city was engulfed in riots because of the lamentation and cries of the people. The priests also called upon their God, and the old men and women and princes covered themselves with ashes and afflicted their minds with fasting. They withheld food even from the young, and milk from the sucklings. They cried to God to guard the treasury and the riches deposited therein. Even the young virgins spread out their hands through the windows of their houses and sought the Lord for protection.

Onias the priest afflicted his mind, stripped himself of his robes of honor, and dressed in sackcloth and ashes, as he was grief-stricken, and, from his appearance, one could imagine the sorrow that was in his heart.

On the next day, the enemy came with all his armies and went into the temple shouting, but the Lord caused a strong and mighty sound of thunder to be heard, together with an earthquake, and a storm that knocked down mountains and shattered rocks. On hearing this, all his soldiers ran away, and hid themselves wherever they could, so that he remained alone, and, lifting up his eyes, he saw a magnificent man clothed in gold, dressed with precious stones, and wearing weapons of war. He was riding a splendid horse, that was plunging and rearing, trotting and galloping in the temple. Heliodorus immediately ran away, but the horse knocked him to the ground and stood over him. The man then commanded his two young servants, clothed in white linen, with staffs in their hands, to beat Heliodorus very severely, and the two young men did as he commanded, one on each side of him, they beat him mercilessly until he became insensible and floated between life and death.

The young priests then came and lifted him on their shoulders, carried him into his tent, and placed him in his bed, where he lay motionless and dumbfounded. He could not speak or eat any food. When the elders of Macedon saw him in this state, they came to Onias the priest, crying and begging him, and aid, "My lord, we beg you, pray for your servant Heliodorus and all his servants who have come with him, that we may live and not die, for we know that there is no other God except yours, since all the gods of the nations are vanity and emptiness, while yours is the God that created the world, and in whose hand is the soul of every living being."

The priest, then praying to God, offered up burnt offerings and sacrifices, and the two young men that beat Heliodorus by the temple appeared to him and said, "Arise, go to Onias the priest, and bow down to his feet, as for his sake the Lord has had mercy on you."

Heliodorus rose up and went to the priest, bowed before him, and blessed the Lord and the priest. He then gave a great deal of gold and silver to the treasury of the temple of the Lord.

Then he rushed back to Macedonia, directly to Seleucus the king, who asked, "What happened in Jerusalem?"

Heliodorus replied, "If you have any enemies who seek your life, send them immediately to Jerusalem, and let them go into the temple, where they will surely be killed, for the great God reigns in that place, and destroys all the enemies of Jerusalem and Judea."

He then told the king all that he had seen, and Seleucus never again sent his army to Jerusalem to do evil, but, on the contrary, every year until his death he sent a gift to the temple, and the kings of the land sent their offerings to honor the temple at Jerusalem.

Chapter 2 Notes

1 Hebrew: Slåwqws (סלאוקוס). Translation: Seleucus

Seleucus IV Philopator (Σέλευκος Φιλοπάτωρ) was the king of the Seleucid Empire from 187 to 175 BC. At that time, the empire covered modern-day Syria, Lebanon, Israel, Palestine, Iraq, Kuwait, southwestern Turkey, and western Iran.

2 Seleucus I Nicator never conquered Macedon. He did conquer all of Alexander's conquered territory other than Egypt, however, died during his invasion of Macedon.

3 Hebrew: Choniyyo (חוֹנִיוֹ)

This high priest is more commonly known as Onias today, based on the Greek spelling of his name: Onais (Ὀνίας).

Chapter 3

Ptolemy[1] the Macedonian, who was made king of Egypt, was a wise and clever king, who loved books. He, therefore, commanded two of his officers to collect many of them. The names of these princes were Aristios and Andrios. Having collected together many Median and Persian books, besides others in all kinds of languages, the king asked them, "How many books have you acquired?"

"Nine hundred and fifty," they replied.

Ptolemy laughed at this, and said, "Go and add another fifty to make a thousand."

But Aristios and Andrios replied, "My lord, it is vanity that we tire ourselves out obtaining these books since they are useless. Now, if it pleases the king, let him write to the priest in Jerusalem, and he will send you some wise men of that place, who know the Greek language, who will explain to you their law, which is the sacred writing, as the books we have copied are of no use."

Acting upon their advice, the king made such a request of the priest in those days, and the high priest sent him seventy priests with Eleazar as their elder. (The same Eleazar who was afterwards tried during the reign of Antiochus, and who died a martyr's death for his God.)

CHAPTER 3

When Eleazar and these seventy priestly interpreters came to Egypt, Ptolemy put them in seventy different houses, each distinct from the other, provided each one with a scribe, and the priests interpreted the whole twenty-four books of the law, which these seventy elders then translated from Hebrew into Greek. As soon as it was finished, Eleazar brought the various copies to the king, who, after reading each one of them, found that they were all the same, and that the interpretations of all were identical.

The king was overjoyed at this, and, presented Eleazar and the seventy elders with a great deal of money, and sent them back to Jerusalem. He also gave 150,000 Judahite men their freedom, besides presenting them each with fifty drachmas of gold,[2] and a table of pure gold weighing 1,000 talents for the temple. Upon it, he engraved the land of Egypt, and the course of the Nile River in Egypt, by which the country is watered, and inlaid it with precious stones. Nothing like it had ever been seen in all the land. King Ptolemy sent this as a present to the temple of the great and awe-inspiring God of the whole world.

Chapter 3 Notes

1 Hebrew: Tlmy (תלמי). Translation: Ptolemy

Ptolemy I Soter (Πτολεμαῖος Σωτήρ) was the Macedonian general who was appointed satrap of Egypt at the Partition of Babylon, in 323 BC. After the imperial regent Perdiccas was killed in 321 BC, Ptolemy was offered the regency of the Macedonian empire until Alexander III's son was old enough to assume the kingship, however, rejected the offer. At the time, the empire was on the verge of collapse, and in the ensuing wars of the Diadochi, Ptolemy managed to secure his kingship over Egypt, Cyrene, Judea, Syria, Cyprus, and Cilicia.

2 The drachma was generally a silver coin, however, gold drachmas were also mentioned in ancient literature. The version of this story in Arabic Maccabees claims it was 'several dinars,' which suggests that this is an older form of the story than the Arabic translation. The Arabic word dynār (دِينَار) was adopted from the Latin term denarius, which was the name of a common coin used in the Roman Empire from 211 BC to 244 AD. The word was also adopted into Greek as dênarion (δηνάριον), Syriac as dynrå (ܕܝܼܢܵܪܐ), and Palestinian Aramaic as dynr (דינרא). The denarius was a low-value coin, the name translating as 'ten.' It was valued at 10 aes, the basic Roman monetary unit. While often compared to the cent or penny due to being made of copper, the aes coin was subdivided into smaller denominations, making the denarius the conceptual equivalent of a modern $10 or £10 bill. While the denarius was already in use by the era of the story, it was not in use in Greek-speaking countries. The Hebrew reference to 50 drachmas would be the equivalent of 5 dinars, indicating the Palestinian Aramaic precursor to Arabic Maccabees, likely used Hebrew Maccabees as a source. Based on internal references, the Aramaic precursor to Arabic Maccabees was composed shortly after 525 AD, likely in Byzantine Palestine, indicating that *Hebrew Maccabees* almost certainly predates that time.

Chapter 4

A long time after this, Antiochus was made King of Macedonia. Meanwhile, Ptolemy, King of Egypt, was gathered to his people, and another Ptolemy succeeded him. Antiochus rose against him, and after killing him, captured the entire land of Egypt, over which he reigned.[1]

In those days, fierce battles began to be fought against the Judahites, for after Antiochus had defeated Egypt he became very proud, and issued a proclamation to every people, commanding them to bow down to the statues of the king. All the nations obeyed, and the godless men of our people, Menelaos, Simeon, Alkimos, and others, incited Antiochus to do evil to the Israelites. At this time a great miracle was seen in Jerusalem. Forty men were seen riding between the sky and the earth on what appeared to be horses made of fire. The riders carried in their hands golden weapons of war, with which they fought one against the other for forty days.

At this, the wicked men of our people went to King Antiochus, and said, "Behold, we have seen a miracle in Jerusalem, and the people say that Antiochus the king is dead, and are rejoicing at the death of our lord."

The king was enraged at this, and immediately went to Jerusalem and killed them with the edge of the sword so that there was a great slaughter in the city. A great multitude of them were sent into exile, and the assembly of the Hasidians[2] scattered. They fled to the forest, fed upon the grass like animals, and hid themselves in the forest like wild beasts, because Antiochus was not satisfied with slaughtering many, and he sent many more into slavery.

When he left the land of Judea, he left his officers to punish the people, and he left Philip Pelusium.[3] He came from the Phrygians,[4] who are also the Thracians,[5] from whom the Romans are also descended from. Philip belonged to that nation. The king left him there to oppress the Israelites, commanding him, "Whoever is willing to bow down to the statue I set up, and to eat of the flesh of the hogs, shall live, but all who refuse shall be killed without mercy. Also don't allow these people to observe the Sabbath, or to circumcise their children."

Chapter 4 Notes

1 None of the kings named Antiochus ever conquered the Ptolemys' Egypt, however, Antiochus IV Epiphanes did soundly defeat the Egyptian army at the Battle of Pelusium, in 173 BC.

2 Hebrew: Chasidim (חֲסִידִים). Translation: pious

The Hasidians were a sect of Judeans that were mentioned in several ancient sources, but died out or changed their name before the time of Josephus, and so little is known of them. In the Septuagint's *1ˢᵗ Maccabees,* the Asidaeoe (Ἀσιδαῖοι) were a sect of Judeans who supported Judas' rebellion. In *2ⁿᵈ Maccabees*, the author claims that Judas was a Hasidian, although this is not supported in other records, including this book. The Vetus Latina book of *Esther* also claims to be the 'Book of Hadassah, which is called Esther,' indicating it was a holy book of the Hasidian sect.

The Arabic translator of *Arabic Maccabees* wrote the following about them, likely earlier than 1200 AD:

> The author of this book did not describe their rules, nor do we know anything of them other than their name, as they applied themselves to practices that were more the eminent virtues, namely, to select from those two other sects whichever was most safe in belief, most sure and guarded.

The nature of the sect is debated by scholars, some viewing them as a precursor to the Pharisees, and others viewing them as either a precursor or alternate name of the Essenes (Ἐσσηνοί) sect, who were mentioned by Josephus and others at the time. The Hebrew word chasidim (חֲסִידִים) translates as the plural form of pious (the 'pious' people), while the Greek name Essenes (Ἐσσηνοί) was defined by Philo of Alexandria circa 40 AD as meaning something like the plural form of 'holy' (the 'holy' people), which does support the connection between the groups. As the Essenes also followed the priesthood of Zedok (צדק), descended from the Solomonic priesthood, they are probably the source of the earliest Christian communities in Judea and Galilee, as the author of the Letter to the Hebrews made it clear that the church in Jerusalem was following the priesthood of Melchizedek, meaning 'King Sdq' (מלכי־צדק). Sdq, also translated as Zedok, Zedek, or Sydyk, was the Canaanite god of justice, similar to the Latin Jupiter.

The Vetus Latina book of *Esther* is significantly closer to both versions of *Esther* found in Septuagint manuscripts than to the abridged version found in the Masoretic texts, suggesting that the Hasidians influenced the development of the Septuagint and Vetus Latina manuscripts. The Masoretic version of Esther has had all references to God removed, indicating that the original text was considered heretical to the Pharisees. The Greek and Old Latin versions refer to God by the name or title 'King,' which would translated back to Hebrew as Mlk (מלך), the same spelling as the name of the god Moloch (מלך), whose worship had been purged under King Josiah circa 625 BC. Moloch is spelled as Mwlk (מולך) in modern literature to distinguish the name from the word for king, however, was spelled the same way as 'king' in the Masoretic texts. He is identified in the Masoretic *Book of Kings* (Septuagint's *3rd Kingdoms*) as being Ammonite and generally accepted as the archeologically attested Ammonite god Milkom (𐤌𐤋𐤊𐤌). Mlkm (𐎎𐎍𐎋𐎎) was also mentioned as a god in the Ugaritic texts from the 1300s BC, indicating that he had been worshiped in Canaan since the Bronze Age.

The Akkadian Cuneiform version of the word mlk (𐤌𐤋𐤊) was malkum ([cuneiform]), meaning 'prince,' a title given to Nergal, the prince of the great city (underworld), and son of Ellil (𒀭𒂗𒆤), which also gave him the title of aplu ^ilu^Ellil ([cuneiform] 𒀭𒂗𒆤), meaning 'son of ^god^Enlil.' In the Old Akkadian flood narrative of Atra-Hasis, Ellil was the god who caused the great flood, and his rival god Ia warned Arta-Hasis that the flood was coming, giving him enough time to build a huge box to shelter in with his family. After this flood, Atra-Hasis emerged from the box, which had floated down the river, and gave thanks to Ellil, Ia, and their father Ilu (god) for sparing his life.

In Syria, the name aplu ^ilu^Ellil ([cuneiform] 𒀭𒂗𒆤) was shortened to Aplu ([cuneiform]) by the Hurrians and adopted as Apaliunas ([cuneiform]) by the Neshites (Hittites). Based on archeological evidence, Apaliunas was also worshipped by the Trojans, meaning that he was the 'Apollo' the Greeks recorded the Trojans worshipping during the Late Bronze Age.

Earlier, during the Middle Bronze Age, the Amorites had called Resheph the 'son of Ellil,' however, after the Hyksos dynasty fell, the Amorite gods were initially suppressed, resulting in Resheph being called Shed ([hieroglyphs]) in the Egyptian controlled parts of Canaan, which translates as 'savior,' as Resheph was believed to spare people from going to the Great City (underworld).

In the 20th century, the prominent biblical scholar William F. Albright proposed that the Canaanite god Melqart (𐤕𐤀𐤐𐤋𐤙) was also a version of this 'Prince of the Underworld,' as his name is generally accepted as originally being Mlk Qrt (𐤕𐤀𐤐 𐤙𐤋𐤙), meaning 'King of the City.' The city in question is usually assumed to be Tyre, however, he was widely worshiped throughout Phoenician colonies, including the colonies of Sidon and Byblos, which were the chief rivals of Tyre. If the 'city' was a reference to the underworld, as it was referred to in Babylonian literature, then Melqart, Milcom, and Moloch would be regional variants of the same Canaanite god of the underworld that Josiah banned the worship of circa 625 BC. As Melqart continued to be worshiped in Carthage and its colonies, there is no reason the banned Ammonite god Moloch would not have been.

In this book Mattathias also called his god 'the king,' however, he later anoints his son Judas in the name of Sabaoth, suggesting he was practicing a form of Judaic polytheism that survived since the time before Josiah's reforms. As the Solomonic priesthood of Sydyk continued to operate in Judea, and was the priesthood of the Hasidians, and the Solomonic tradition was polytheistic, it suggests that Mattathias was a Hasidian priest.

There are no other references to the Hasidian sect continuing to exist after the Maccabean Revolt, and 1st

Maccabees describes them being killed on the Sabbath as they refused to fight when attacked.

There was a German Jewish sect that used the name 'Hasidian' in the 1300s, however, they are generally not accepted as being descended from the Classical era Hasidians. The gap between the Judean Hasidians and German Hasidians is over a thousand years, making the word 'Hasidian' in the text anomalous. In the other books of the Maccabees, the word 'Hasidian' is generally only used once or twice. This seems to have been because the Greek and Arabic translators did not understand the term, while the Hebrew translator did.

3 Hebrew: Pylypws Plwsywm (פיליפוס הפלוסיום). Translation: Philip Pelusium

Philip is not otherwise identified as coming from Pelusium, a city in eastern Egypt. This was likely an honorific title because he fought at the battle of Pelusium in 173 BC when Antiochus IV Epiphanes defeated the armies of Ptolemy VI Philometor. After he withdrew from the rest of Egypt, Pelusium remained a Seleucid city within Egypt.

4 Hebrew: Prygy (פריגי). Translation: Phrygia

5 Hebrew: Tryygy (תרייגי)

The meaning of this word has been debated as it is not a known Hebrew language toponym. In the 1800s, it was interpreted as 'Trojans' based on context, however, this is

unlikely as the Hebrew spelling of Trojans is Trwånm
(טרויאנים). The word is probably a transliteration of the Punic
name for Thace: Tryygy (𐤕𐤓𐤉𐤉𐤂𐤉). Most modern forms of
'Thace' are derived from the Greek Thracê (Θρᾴκη),
including the Modern Hebrew Tråkyh (תראקיה). Conversely,
the Punic form of the name was adopted earlier, and
independent from Greek influence, as the Phoenicians had
trading colonies in Thrace by 800 BC. Due to the close trade
connections between the Carthaginians and Celtiberians, the
Punic name was adopted into Celtic languages, and survived
as late as the 700s AD in the Old Celtic form of the name:
Traigia (ᛟ ᛟᛟᛟᛟ᛭ᛟᛟᛟᛟ᛭᛭ᛟᛟᛟᛟ᛭). This was updated to the Greek-
influenced Tráicia after the Latin alphabet became dominant.
While the Romans are not accepted today as being descended
from Thracians, the Phrygians are believed to have been an
offshoot of the Thracians, based on linguistic analysis, and
similar religious beliefs. As the Romans are also not believed
to have been related to the Trojans, the translation of
'Thracians' is used.

Chapter 5

The king then returned to Macedonia, and, having left Philip in the land of Judea. He followed the word of the king and prohibited the Judahites from studying the Torah and from performing the service of their God. He supported the wicked and the rebellious of our people and slaughtered many of the assembly of the Hasidians.

At that time two women were discovered who had circumcised their children. They hanged them by their breasts and then hurled them with their children from the top of a tower. They burst open and died.

After this Eleazar, the high priest, who we have mentioned as having gone to Egypt in the days of Ptolemy, was captured and brought to Philip. Philip said to him, "Eleazar, you are a wise man and a man of understanding, now, do not disobey the command of the king, but eat of the meat of his sacrifice."

But Eleazar replied, "Far be it from me to set aside the command of my God in order to follow the command of the king."

Then Philip called him aside and said, "You know that I have loved you for many years, therefore I have pity for your mind and for your old age. Let a portion of the flesh of your own sacrifices which you are allowed to eat be brought to you, and eat it before the people so that they will say you eat of the flesh of the king's sacrifice. Through this, you can save your life and not die."

When Eleazar heard this he thought of the greatness of his honor and of the sanctity of his glory, and said to Philip, "I am now ninety years old, and have never yet served my God in deceit, nor is it appropriate for me to do so now, and to deceive men, as then the young men will say, 'Since Eleazar, although being ninety years old, has abandoned the law of his God, we can also do so,' and they will bring destruction upon themselves. Now, far be it from me to defile my holiness, to taint the purity of my old age, and to cause these young men with me to waver, and give them the pretext for saying, 'Eleazar, although being ninety years old, has sinned against his God, and has chosen to serve the vanities of the nations, so let us do the same.' Even if I escape from your hands today, I cannot escape God. No man can, either living or dead since His dominion extends over the living to bring death upon them, and over the dead to resurrect them to life. I will therefore die true in my faith, and wall leave my power behind to my people and my young men so that when they see me give up my life so readily, they will desire to follow my example, and thus keep their Torah precious, and will choose a worthy death."

When Philip heard these words, he became exceedingly cruel and commanded his men to tie up the pious old man, and to beat him. They therefore beat him with all manner of weapons mercilessly, and he groaned, saying, "Lord my God, who has caused me to reach this old age, You know that I was able to save my mind from such a death, but did not wish to do so on account of my love for You. Now they beat me so cruelly and fiercely that I would not be able to bear it were it not for my fear of You, which renders them as nothing in my eyes, and I suffer them willingly."

While he was still speaking these words his life ended, and he left strength to his people and power to his young men.

Chapter 6

Seven brothers and their mother were then arrested and sent to the king, for the king had not yet left Jerusalem. Because pork was abhorred by the Judeans, and stank, and was despised by them, the cruelties against them were increased, and he tore their flesh like that of an ox.

When the first son was brought before the king, he said, "Why waste words to teach us, when we have already been taught by our forefathers? We are prepared to suffer death for the Lord and His law."

The king was furious at this and ordered a brass pan be brought, and placed it on the fire. Then, he ordered his tongue to be cut out, his hands and legs, and the skin of his head to be cut off, he placed them all in the frying pan in front of his brothers. The rest of his body they threw into a large brass pot that was placed on the hot coals. When he was near death the king commanded the fire to be removed from under the pot so that he should not die too quickly, in order to terrify his brothers and his mother. However, the opposite happened, and they encouraged each other and fortified each other when they saw that their brother gave up his life for the Lord and His Torah, and said to each other, "See what Moses, the servant of the Lord, said in his song, 'He shall be comforted in His servants.' Now the Lord is comforted in us for all the evil which He has purposed to do to His people, and He will have compassion upon them.'"

As soon as the first died, the second brother was brought. They said to him, "Listen to the command of the king. Why die in great torture like your brother?"

However, he replied, "Prepare your sword and fire, and do not do less to me than you did to my brother, as I do not fall short of my brother in piety and the fear of God."

Every limb was then commanded to be cut off and placed in the frying pan on the fire. He then said, "Hear me, you cruel king. Are you able to tie up our minds which you steal from us? Know that they will walk to God, who has given them to us, to the light that is the Lord. We will again live a life that has no limit or end when He awakens the dead of His people and the murdered of His servants."

Then the second brother died.

When the third was brought, he looked at the king, and, stretching out his right hand towards the king, said, "What business of yours is it to destroy us, you enemy and foe? All this comes from the sky, and we receive it with love. Your tortures are despicable in our eyes, and are nothing to us as we expect honor and favor from the sky. He will grant us the reward for our actions."

The king and all his princes were astonished at the bravery of the youth. After his death, the fourth brother was brought.

"What," he asked, "have I to do with you, you evil man? We die for the Lord, and He will again bring us back to life, but you shall never rise again."

When the fifth was brought, he said, "Do not imagine that God has forgotten us, for on account of His great love has He brought us to this honor. You reviler and blasphemer, the Lord hates you and stirs you up to do to us whatever you want, but a great vengeance will be taken upon you and your descendants, and His anger will be kindled against you and all your family."

After his death, the sixth brother was brought before the king, who said, "We know our wickedness, for we have sinned against the Lord, and now our minds are given over to death as an atonement for our people. But now, because your heart prompts you to do this thing to the servants of our God and to fight against God, know that He shall fight against you and uproot you from the face of the earth."

The seventh and last brother was only a young boy, yet the mother, who had seen her seven sons killed on one day, did not fear nor tremble, but, standing upright by the corpses of her sons, she raised her voice and shouted, "My son! My son! I do not know how you were formed in my womb, nor did I give you the breath and soul which you had, nor bring you out of my womb, nor raise you, nor make you grow, or your flesh which is now offered as a sacrifice, God formed it. He wove the sinews and covered it with skin, and caused hair to grow upon it. He then breathed in your nostrils the breath of life. Since you give up all this for His sake, He will restore them to you and will renew your body. He will give you the reward of your actions, and happy are you, my sons, for all this."

At this, the king was very surprised, as the woman had humbled him.

"Bring me the seventh one," he ordered, "Perhaps, as he is but a young boy, I may be able to convince him with soft words to do our will. Do not let this woman boast of me, saying, 'I have defeated King Antiochus in convincing my sons to die for our God.'"

Following the king's command, the seventh boy was brought, and the king implored him and took an oath to enrich him with silver and gold, with cattle and many servants, to make him viceroy, and to let him rule over the whole kingdom. But the boy despised the words of the king, and the king summoned the mother to him, and said, "Good woman, have pity on this child, and be merciful to the fruit of your womb. Induce him to do my will and to be spared."

The woman answered, "Give him to me, and I will convince him with kind words."

When this was done, she led him aside, kissed him, and celebrated at the king's shame and confusion. She said, "My son, you whom I carried in my womb for nine months, and whom I suckled for three years, and after which I sustained you with food until this very day, give up all this offered honor, and fear the God that I taught you about. My son, look toward the sky and see the land, the sea, the waters, and the fire, which were created by the word of the Lord. Man is simply flesh and blood and nothing before Him. Do not be afraid of this cruel man, but give up your life for the sake of the Lord. Go the same way as your brothers. If only I could see where your brothers are now, and the greatness of their glory before the Lord. My son, cling to your brothers, and your fate will be like their glory. I will go there with you, and celebrate with you as on the days of your marriage. I will be with you in your righteousness."

While she was still speaking the boy answered, and said, "Why do you delay me, and will not let me go and join my holy brothers? I will not listen to the king, but to the law of our God, which He has given through the hand of Moses to the people of Israel, which this cruel enemy of God has put to shame and reviled. Woe to you! Woe to you! Where will you go? Where will you flee? Where will you run? Where will you hide yourself from our God, oh enemy, foe, and wicked man, for He still keeps us alive, and has glorified and exalted us over all nations? But you who are insolent enough to stretch out your hand against His servants, it would be better for you if you had not been born."

"You wicked fool Antiochus, who was begotten of tainted folly, has committed evil against yourself. You have done good to us, and if we endure and bear these tortures in this world, we will be taken to the life and light of the world where there is no darkness, but eternal life without death. You will be the abomination of all creatures and will be abhorred by our God when He takes vengeance upon you. You will die an unnatural death, plagued with dreadful diseases. You will descend to the bottom of Gehenna.[1] You will be drawn into darkness, where there is no life or light, but darkness and shades, where there is no repose or rest, but trouble, sorrow, brimstone, and fire. This will be your inheritance from the Lord and your lot from our God, you man of blood and wicked man."

"God will have mercy upon His people. Until now His wrath has rested upon us, but He will no longer be angry with His people but will repent for what He has done to us before, although He did so in truth and in righteousness, as we had acted wickedly. He will return and have mercy upon us, and will grant us eternal life."

King Antiochus now became extremely angry because he would not obey his will, and therefore increased the tortures, and acted more cruelly to him than he had to the others.

The seventh died like this.

The mother stood by the corpses of her sons, and, spread out her hands, saying, "Exalted and awe-inspiring God! God of the universe! I will come now! I will die now with my sons in the place which You have prepared for them."

While she was still speaking she finished her days upon earth, falling upon the dead bodies of her sons, her breath went out, and she died with them.

Chapter 6 Notes

1 Aramaic: gyhnwm (גיהנום)

In the Classical era, Geyhinŵm (גֵּיהִנּוֹם) was interpreted as the underworld, a vague equivalent of the Greek Hades. The Greek transliteration of geenna (γέεννα) and Latin transliteration of gehenna were adopted during the Classical era by both Jews and Christians.

The older Hebrew term used in Masoretic Joshua was gy vn hnm (גי בן הנם), meaning 'gorge of sons of Hinns,' which explained in a scribal note as asher be'emek refa'im tzafovnah (אֲשֶׁר בְּעֵמֶק רְפָאִים צָפוֹנָה), meaning 'which is the depths of Raphaim of the north.' The Raphiam were mentioned in the Ugaritic texts of northern Canaan from the mid-1300s BC as Rpm (𒊑𒉿𒈨), which were depicted as princes ruling in the underworld.

The origin of the name Hnm (הנם) is likely a plural of hinn (حِنّ), a reference to an ancient extinct type of being that once lived on the Earth in Semitic folklore. The hinns continue to be part of the Islamic and Druze religions, although their roles in the religions vary. It is agreed that they are extinct, however, it isn't clear what they were. Many sources describe the hinns and binns as powerful, gigantic primordial creatures, suggesting they were influenced by finding the bones of extinct animals. Conversely, the *Revelations of 'Abdullah Al-Sayid Muhammad Habib* claims the hinns were air creatures, and the binns were water creatures, while the medieval Islamic historian al-Tabari claimed they were created from poisonous fire (سموم). In most versions of the stories, they fought in part of a series of wars for control of the earth before the creation of humanity, and most of the ancient species became extinct, including the hinns.

Chapter 7

The king then continued on his way to Macedon, and commanded Philip and the captains that he had left in the land of Judea, "Blot out the very memory of Judea from the face of the earth, and let he who but mentions the name 'Judea' be killed. Let all those live who are willing to be assimilated with our people, and be called 'Javan.'"

Therefore, Philip and the captains with him destroyed everyone he discovered observing the Torah, with the exception of those who fled with Mattathias ben John[1] to Modi'in. Mattathias could not bear the insults of the uncircumcised, but was zealous for his God, and wept, stating, "Woe to me, my mother who gave me birth to see the breach of my people."

He sent his son Judas secretly to tell the Judeans, "Whoever of you are on the side of the Lord, come to me."

A large assembly of Hasidians gathered around him, and Mattathias said to them, "Why waste words? The only thing that remains for us to do is to pray and fight. Let us strengthen ourselves and die in battle, but not be like sheep led to slaughter."

When they heard these words, all of them became encouraged, and each one said to another, "To your tent, Judah! Rule over your own land again! Enough of King

Antiochus! Now sharpen your sword, Judahites! Beware of your life, Macedonians!"

From that day the Macedonian yoke was broken from the shoulders of Judea.

When Philip and the generals of the king heard these words they went out against them with a large army. As they were going against them, they found a cave on the way filled with Judean men, women, and children, all observing the Sabbath. They approached the entrance of the cave, and said to them, "Come out and profane the Sabbath. Follow the command of the king and live. Don't allow yourselves to die!"

They replied, "We won't come out, nor will we profane the Sabbath day. Let the sky and the earth be witness that we die in our integrity."

Then Philip commanded fire to be brought and placed at the mouth of the cave. Then he placed some wood on it. He filled the cave with smoke and they all suffocated.

The generals of the king then marched against Mattathias, to Mount Modi'in, and found him, his sons, his brothers, and some of his people from the assembly of the Hasidians fully armed for war, as they had brought their wives and children to that mountain. The generals of the king approached Mattathias with peaceful words, saying, "Oh, honored among your people, follow the command of the king and live and do not die."

Mattathias answered very proudly, "I obey the command of my king.[2] You obey the command of yours."

The generals were confused by this and became silent. They did not say another word, as they wondered about the sanity of Mattathias, and were considering how they could capture and kill him as they had slain the other pious men.

Suddenly one of the renegade Judeans with the generals of the king said, "I am surprised at the generals of the king and his army. How long will you hold your peace and not follow the command of the king by rising up against Mattathias, who was insolent enough to refuse to obey the king's command?"

After he said this, he unsheathed his sword, cut off the head of a hog, picked it up with his hands, and carried it to the altar that they had built to sacrifice to the king's idols. Then, placing the head of the hog on the altar, he sacrificed it with frankincense to the idol of Antiochus.

When Mattathias saw this he was enraged, and his fury burned within him. He drew his sword and leaped at the sacrificing Judean, and severed his head from his body. He held it up high before the generals of the king who were near Mattathias, while the body fell down from the altar upon which he had stood. He also killed one of the king's generals, which caused the rest of them to run, knocking to the ground many of the crowd. Then he blew the shofar, giving the signal for war. He was the first one to raise his hand against the Macedonian kingdom.

(He also commanded us to fight on the Sabbath, and he will stand by us to defend us in this matter. This is written in the book of Joseph ben Gurion, the priest.)

Mattathias with his sons and brothers then marched out, and with them a large band of the Hasidians. They pursued those who had hidden themselves, and killed and tortured them until there was not one remaining in the whole land of Judea. They then circumcised their sons. Thus, great salvation was brought about by the Lord through Mattathias.

Chapter 7 Notes

1 Hebrew: Mattityahu ben Yochanan (מַתִּתְיָהוּ בֶּן יוֹחָנָן).

Mattityahu is the generally known as Mattathias the son of John from the Greek translation of his name.

2 Hebrew: mlky (מלכי). Translation: my king

The word 'king' was used as a name or title of God or a god by the Hasidian sect of Judaism in the early Second Temple era, suggesting that Mattathias was a Hasidian.

Chapter 8

When the days of Mattathias were drawing to a close, he called his five sons to his bedside and encouraged them and exhorted them, saying, "I know that now terrible battles will be waged in the land of Judea, since we have been stirred up to fight for our nation. Now, my sons, be zealous for your God, and for His temple, and for His people. Fight, and do not be afraid of death. If you die in battle, you will be resurrected among your brothers, and their inheritance will be shared with you, for all our ancestors who have been zealous for God, God has given honor and favor. Didn't our ancestor Pinehas receive the eternal covenant, and did not our other ancestors who were zealous for the Lord receive their reward from the Lord?"

Then he said to Simeon his son, "I know the wisdom that God has put in your heart. Don't withhold it. Counsel your people, and be to your brothers like a father, and they will listen to you and to all your counsel since our God has given you strength and wisdom."

Next Mattathias called his son Judas, who came and stood before him, and he said, "My son Judas, who is called the hammer[1] because of your strength. I know, my son, that you are a warrior, and that God has given you strength and might, and a heart like a lion's that runs from nothing. Now, my son, honor the Lord with all the strength the Lord has granted you. Fight His battles without stopping. Don't be reluctant to travel the four corners of the land: the east, west, south, and north, to capture the country from the power of the uncircumcised. Be the captain of their army and the anointed of battle."

Then he brought out a horn of oil and poured it upon his head, anointing him for Sabaoth,[2] while all the people shouted loudly, blew their trumpets, and cried out, "Long live the anointed!"

When he had finished his speech to his sons, he died and was gathered to his people, and Judas his son, nicknamed Maccabee, rose in his place. He had the help of his brothers, his father's household, and all the assembly of the Hasidians.

Judas enjoyed fighting the battles of Israel. He dressed himself in a coat of mail like a warrior and equipped himself with the weapons of war. He looked like one of the sons of Anak. He protected the camp of Israel with his sword and pursued the enemy, and he stomped out their life. He burnt the sinners with the fire of his mouth, confounded the wicked with terror, and confused all the sinners through fear of him, as he appeared to them just as a roaring lion seeking prey appears to cattle.

CHAPTER 8

Jacob rejoiced at his accomplishments and was glad at his actions, for he confounded great kings, so that his name was celebrated from one end of the world to the other, and people constantly spoke of the wars he waged. Blessed is his name among the people of Israel. Peace and repose be on his righteous couch, and blessing on his holy bed, for he did not withhold his mind from death to defend Israel, God's people, and has slain all the wicked Judahites who led the Israelites astray.

When Apollonius, the commander of the Macedonian army, heard these things, he said, "Who is it that dared to rebel against our lord the king?"

He amassed around himself a large and strong multitude of Macedonian warriors and marched forward to fight against Israel. Judas went out to meet him, and a very fierce battle took place between the Macedonians and the assembly of the Hasidians. During the battle, Judas saw Apollonius standing in the middle of the Macedonian company, and ran towards him in the fury of his anger, killing to the right and left and in front of him. He cut down the mighty Greek men, just like the reaper cuts down the sheaves and the corn of his harvest. Then, approaching Apollonius, he killed him with the edge of the sword and knocked him to the ground. The Greeks and Macedonians turned and fled quickly, and Judas and the assembly of the Hasidians pursued them and killed them in a very great slaughter. When they captured their spoils, Judas seized Apollonius' sword and fought with it all his life.

When Seron, the captain of the army of Syria, heard this he said, "I will go and fight against Judas, and make a name for myself."

Then Judas ben Mattathias summoned all his people, and he marched to Beth-Horon. Judas became aware of this, and said to his men, "There is no time to delay. Let's go out to them, although our brothers the Hasidians have gone away from us, as if we wait until they return, our enemies will say we are afraid of them."

Judas marched all night long, and at dawn, when the people suddenly saw in the distance a strong and mighty army, they asked Judas, "How can we who are so few go to war against this great multitude?"

Judas answered, "Pray to the sky, and you will be saved, for the battle is in the hands of the Lord to deliver the many into the hands of the few. It is in His power to save either a multitude or a few."

Then Judas sneaked into the enemy's camp and suddenly attacked them. He struck terror into them, and Seron with all his men became confused. Judas chased him, caught him, and killed him. On that day as many as 800 corpses of the Syrians were found piled up in heaps on the field. Those who remained fled into the land of the Philistines, and the fear of Judas fell upon all the nations.

When Antiochus heard this, he was very angry and gathered together all his people and all the nations under his rule. He assembled a strong and mighty army and divided it into two divisions. With one half he traveled to (Parthia),[3] as the Persians had revolted from the Macedonian rule when they saw that the Judahites had rebelled. The other half he handed over to Lysias, of his own family, and of royal Macedonian descent, saying to him, "You know everything that Judas ben Mattathias, has done to my two generals: Apollonius and Seron, and to all their army. Therefore, go now and kill all the inhabitants of Judea, and my son Eupator will go with you. I myself will go to Persia and uproot the nation that rebelled against me."

Then King Antiochus went to Persia and left Lysias in command to wage war against Judea and look after his son. Lysias chose for himself Tolmios[4] (who is Ptolemy), Nicanor, and Gorgias, men of valor, sending with them 40,000 young warriors on foot and 7,000 cavalrymen, and the entire armies of both Syria and Philistia joined them in marching against Judea to destroy it. When Judas and all the elders of Israel heard this they proclaimed a fast, clothed themselves in sackcloth, and placing dust upon their heads, cried unto the Lord.

After the fast, Judas counted his people and appointed over them captains of thousands, captains of hundreds, captains of fifties, and captains of tens. Then they marched into the field, and he issued an order to the camp, saying, "Whoever has planted a vineyard or built a house, and whoever is engaged to be married or fearful, let him return home," and many of them left. There remained 7,000 valiant men, chosen warriors, none of which would have run away before a hundred enemies.

Judas then marched on to meet Nicanor, who had brought many merchants with him, as he intended to sell to them the young men and women that he was going to capture and sell them into slavery from Judea. He went into the valley to meet Judas. Judas came out of the assembly of the Hasidians who were with him, and called upon the Lord, saying, "Exalted God, who has ruled from the creation until now, who causes battles to end, and in whose hands is power and might to exalt or to humble, subdue and humble this nation before the lowly of Your people, for You will subdue nations under us and peoples under our feet."

After his prayer, the priests blew their holy trumpets, and all the people shouted. Then Judas raced into battle and attacked the camp of Nicanor slaughtering so many that they fled before him. Pursuing them with his army, he continued to kill them as they ran. The number of the dead was 9,000. They then returned and took their plunder and the gold that the merchants had brought with them to purchase the Israelite youths. This they distributed among the poor, and then rested in that place, for the battle that was to be fought on the sixth day.

After leaving there, Judas marched against Bacchides and Timothy,[5] and a severe battle followed between them in which he himself killed twenty Macedonian warriors on that day. Bacchides and Timothy fled and Judas chased them, but he could not capture them as they went to Ashtaroth Karnaim. But he captured Philip, the man who had done so much evil in Judea. When Judas approached him, he turned and ran into a nearby house. Then Judas ordered his men to pull down the house on top of him and to burn him to death in that place. In this, he avenged the death of Eleazar and the blood of those pious men that Philip had shed. They then returned to pillage the dead and they sent the spoils to Jerusalem.

Nicanor fled from there and escaped by removing his purple robe and wearing a poor man's robe so that he would not be recognized. He returned to Macedon like this, and told Lysias all that had happened.

Chapter 8 Notes

1 Aramaic: mkbyy (מכביי)

This is generally accepted as the Hebrew spelling of the Aramaic word mkkbå (𐡌𐡊𐡊𐡁𐡀), meaning 'hammer.'

2 Hebrew: ṣbåwt (צבאות). Translation: wars (or battles, militaries, mobs)

Judas is repeatedly referred to as the 'anointed of ṣbåwt,' suggesting this is the Hebrew or Aramaic name of the Judahite god the Greeks called Sabaoth (Σαβαώθ). In Aramaic, ṣbåwt (צבאות) translates as 'desires,' which completely alters the interpretation of the otherwise Hebrew text, making Judas the 'Anointed of Desires' instead of the 'Anointed of Wars.'

The Greeks interpreted Sabaoth as the Judahite version of the Phrygian god Sabazdiôs (𐊖𐊠𐊁𐊠𐊗𐊜𐊗𐊖), and both local versions of Dionysus (Διόνυσος). In *2ⁿᵈ Maccabees*, Dionysus is used as the proper name of the god worshiped in the temple in Jerusalem under Greek rule. Philip the Phrygian was appointed as the high priest of the temple in Jerusalem, as the Phygians and Judeans were believed to have been worshipping the same god. The descriptions of the interior of the second temple include carvings of grapevines, a sacred fruit in the Dionysian cults, and historians like Josephus recorded seeing the 'vineyard of gold' that had once been in the temple, before being gifted to Rome. The 'vineyard of gold' was originally made by one of the Hasmonean kings, suggesting that the cult of Dionysus continued under

Hasmonean rule, and the real problem was the foreign high priest Philip, not the foreign god.

3 The name of the place he marched to is missing, as if the translator intended to return and fill in the name after looking it up. The campaign in question was against the Parthians, however, the king later returned from the 'land of Ecbatana,' suggesting this may have been the missing word. Ecbatana was the ancient capital of the Medes, and later one of the Persian capital cities. In the era of the story, it was one of the Parthian capitals.

4 Aramaic: Twlmåws (תולמאוס)

The name is an Aramaic transliteration of the Greek name Ptolemaeos (Πτολεμαῖος), however, it is clarified as being 'Ptolemy' (תלמי) in the short scribal note that followed. This, and similar Aramaic names and words in the otherwise Hebrew text indicate it was translated from Aramaic.

5 Aramaic: Bkyrs wTymwtyåws (בכירס וטימותיאוס).
Translation: Bakirs and Timotheos

Tymwtyåws (טימותיאוס) is the Aramaic spelling of the Greek name Timotheos (Τιμόθεος), supporting the Hebrew translation being made from an Aramaic text. The name Bkyrs (בכירס) is clearly a reference to Bacchidês (Βακχίδης) from 1st and 2nd Maccabees, with a scribal error where Bcyds (בכידס) was miscopied as Bcyrs (בכירס). Bacchidês was the military commander of Jerusalem at the time according to Josephus, while Timotheos was the military commander of the garrison in Amman. This spelling of Bkyrs (בכירס) is similar to the spelling of Bkyrws (ܒܟܝܪܘܣ) used in the Syriac translation of *2ⁿᵈ Maccabees*, suggesting the error was in an Aramaic translation of that book that was used as both the source for the Syriac Bible and Hebrew Maccabees. Bacchidês' name was also spelled strangely in the Megillat Antiochus as Bagris (בַּגְרִיס). The Megillat Antiochus is believed to have been composed in Aramaic in Syria, around the year 200 AD, indicating that the name was already generally corrupted in Jewish literature. Like Hebrew Maccabees, the Megillat Antiochus was later translated into Hebrew, likely by the Iberian Jews.

Chapter 9

At that time, King Antiochus returned from Persia, ashamed that the Persians had made him flee the land of Ecbatana, and when he was informed of all that Judas had done to his generals, and how he had killed them, he was filled with fury and rage. He swore and blasphemed, and said, "I will go to Jerusalem, and make it a cemetery, and will fill it with the corpses of the dead."

He then called together all his people, his charioteers and cavalrymen, a large and mighty multitude. But the Lord was jealously protective of His people, of His city, and His temple, and remembered all the evil Antiochus did to His people, He required the blood of those pious men from Antiochus and therefore plagued him with boils and with an internal disease. Yet he was not humbled by this, but said, "Press on, you charioteers! Press on, you cavalrymen! Press on, you soldiers. I will go to Jerusalem, and will carry out my plans, for who can stand before me? Is not the sea and the dry land mine, to change existence according to my will? Can I not transform the earth into the sea and the sea into earth?"

When he had finished saying this he mounted his chariot and traveled with his huge army towards Jerusalem. With him were many elephants, and his camp was enormous. While on the journey, his chariot happened to pass in front of one of the elephants, and it trumpeted.

His horses were startled and ran away from the elephant overturning the chariot, and throwing Antiochus out of it. As a result of the fall, his bones were broken, as he was a stout and very heavy man. The Lord, however, pilled up plagues upon him, and his flesh stank. The stench of his body was like that of a dead man lying in a field at the height of the summer. As soon as his servants lifted him upon their shoulders, they had to drop him back again to the ground and run away, as they could not possibly approach him or carry him because of the dreadful stench of the flesh of that reviler, and blasphemer, and enemy of God.

When his army became tired, and he had become so sick of the stench coming from his body that he wished he could die, he knew then that the hand of the Lord had touched him, and being humbled and made lowly, he said, "The Lord is righteous, who humbles the proud and humiliates the wicked like me, for I have done all this evil to His people and to His pious men. It is for this that all these evils have overtaken me."

He then vowed, "If the Lord will heal me from this disease, I will go to Jerusalem and fill it with silver and gold. I will spread purple carpets in all the streets and will give all my treasury to the temple of the great God. I will circumcise my foreskin, and will go around to all lands exclaiming in a loud voice, 'There is no God in the whole world like the God of Israel.'"

But the Lord did not listen to his prayer, nor did He give ear to him, because along the way as Antiochus the Cruel was traveling, his flesh fell off from his bones until finally, his bowels fell out upon the ground. This is how he died. He died in shame and disgrace and in a strange land. Eupator, his son, succeeded him.

Chapter 10

Judas ben Mattathias, and the assembly of the Hasidians with him, went to Jerusalem and pulled down the altars that the uncircumcised had built. They cleansed the temple of the abominations of the nations and built a new altar. They placed on it the flesh of the sacrifice and arranged the wood, but they could not find the sacred fire.

Then they called upon the Lord through prayer, and fire came out of a stone on the altar, and they placed the wood on it. This fire remained with them until the time of the third captivity. On the 25th of Kislev, they dedicated the altar, placed the showbread in its place, and lit the lights. They praised the name of the Lord by reading the 'Hallel Psalms' for eight days.

Chapter 11

After this dedication, Judas marched to the land of Edom, and Gorgias came to meet him with a huge multitude of men, but Judas attacked Gorgias and his camp, and caused them all to flee. Judas' men pursued them and left 20,000 dead enemies on the field that day.

Gorgias fled to Timothy in Arabia, and Timothy marched out with an army of 120,000 Macedonians and Arabs. He went into the land of Gad and Gilead, and killed many of the Judeans that they sent a letter to Judas, asking, "Come and save us, as the sword of Timothy is consuming us."

Another letter also arrived, reporting, "The sword of Tyre and Sidon is destroying us, and the Macedonians who live there."

As soon as Judas had heard these words, he cried to the Lord, fasted, and prayed. Then he selected all the valiant men and the Hasidians, and he rushed to cross the Jordan. Simeon also took with him 3,000 Judeans and rushed to Galilee, where he engaged in a fierce battle and killed 8,000 men. He saved his brothers in Galilee, then, pillaged the corpses and returned to Jerusalem.

Judas the Anointed one of Sabaoth crossed over the Jordan and arrived in Gilead, where they found Timothy attacking the city on Mount Gilead. They girded himself for combat and a fierce battle followed.

The two armies stood opposing each other, Timothy's being mightier and stronger, while Judas' army was few in number. During the fight, Judas cried out to the Lord, and he suddenly saw five young cavalrymen, dressed in gold. Two of them stood in front of Judas, then situated themselves on each side of him, and protected him with their shields, while the other three fought against the army of Timothy. As soon as Judas saw them, he immediately knew that they were sent from the sky to assist the Hasidians and encourage his men. He pressed hard upon Timothy's army and killed 20,500 of his men. Timothy himself, along with his army fled from there towards the Jordan, but Judas went after him wreaking havoc among them all the way to Gaza.

Timothy recruited more men there and prepared for another battle, and the whole army of Philistia joined his ranks. When Judas arrived at that place he leaped on them like a lion on a flock of sheep. Timothy fleed and his whole army scattered in confusion. The Hasmoneans pursued them and cut them to pieces until there were none left. Timothy fled into Gaza, took refuge within it, and closed the gates of the city. From the high walls, he continued to battle for five days as Judas and his men besieged it.

On the fifth day, Timothy's men climbed the high tower, cursed and defiled the Anointed one of Sabaoth, and taunted them all with insolent words. After some time, twenty Hasmoneans became enraged because of the insults. They took their shields in their left hands and their swords in their right hands. They ran towards the wall, climbed the ladder one after another, and attacked those on the wall. They made room for their comrades, all of whom likewise scaled the wall. The twenty men then went into the marketplace of the city, shouting and killing many of the enemies. Then they went towards the gate, and they attacked it from within the city while the whole army of the Hasmoneans approached it from outside. They set it on fire, and the gate collapsed to the ground. This was how the city of Gaza was captured. Then they seized the men who had insulted the Anointed one of Sabaoth and they burnt them to death. After they put the rest of the inhabitants to the edge of the sword. For two whole days, they did not take a break from their work of slaughtering the people.

Timothy ran and hid himself in one of the pits, and so could not be found. But they found his brothers, Birean and Apollopanis, and brought them to Judas, who ordered their heads to be cut off. The plunder of the city they took back to Jerusalem with songs, praises, and thanksgivings, and sang the Psalms of David, King of Israel, to the Lord, whose mercy endures forever.

Chapter 12

When this was heard by Antiochus Eupator, the son of Antiochus Epiphanes, who had done so much evil in Jerusalem, who had killed the Hasidians men, and who ultimately died from the severe plagues inflicted upon him, as we have previously described, this Antiochus Eupator sent Lysias, his cousin, with an army of 80,000 cavalrymen and eighty elephants, a mighty army. They traveled to Judea and Jerusalem and attacked at Beth-Zur.[1] They dug a trench around the city and then began to attack the city with a battering ram and with stones, while Judas and the entire Hasmonean army was camped in the forests and on the mountains far away from the Greek army.

Judas said to his men, "Come, let's approach the Lord our God in fasting and in supplication, and then let's march against the Greek army of Javan, that is attacking Beth-Zur."

After the fast, he blew the shofar and gave the signal for battle. Then he led all his men to assist their brothers in Beth-Zur. When they passed Jerusalem, they entered the temple, offered peace offerings, sacrificed burnt offerings, and cried to the Lord. Then they departed from Jerusalem and traveled to Beth-Zur. Approaching the Macedonian camp, Judas said to his men, "Be strong and cheerful for the people of the Lord! For our brothers, we would rather die together fighting than see any evil fall upon our people."

When he had finished speaking, he lifted up his eyes and saw between heaven and earth a man, well dressed, riding a horse that looked like a flame of fire, and in his hand was a spear. His back was turned towards the Hasmoneans and his face to the camp of the Greeks, with his hand stretched out ready to destroy it. Judas then exclaimed, "Blessed be He who has sent His messenger to save His people and destroy the camp of His enemies."

They rushed towards Beth-Zur, and ran into the Macedonian camp, causing them great confusion, and slaughtered 11,000 infantry and 1,600 cavalrymen. Lysias and his men fled for their lives shamelessly disorganized. Lysias then understood that God was fighting against the enemies of Israel, and made a covenant with Judas.

The following is the letter which Lysias sent to the Judeans:

> Lysias, commander of the king's army and vicegerent of Antiochus, to Judas the Anointed of Sabaoth and to all his people, greeting!

> Let it be known to you that I have received letters you sent through your messengers John and Absalom, and that I have carried out whatever they told me. I read the letter with good feeling and have fulfilled everything contained

therein. I have told the king the message on your behalf, and have given an answer to John and Absalom. I have further charged the messengers I sent to you with words of peace.

This is the contents of the letter that the king sent to his cousin Lysias:

King Antiochus to Lysias, my brother, greetings!

Let it be known to you that we have received the letter you sent us concerning the Judeans and that we have read it with every good feeling. My father has gone the way of all flesh, he has ceased to be with men and has been by with messengers. I wish, for the good of my kingdom, for wars to stop, and to establish peace. I have heard that the Judeans refused to listen to my father to violate their law and that they have therefore conquered by the sword, and killed the prominent men and the most honored of my father's kingdom. Now give them your right hand, and make a covenant with them that they may know it to be my will and my hearty desire that they live in peace and observe their law according to their own wish.

This is the contents of the letter that the king sent to Judas:

King Antiochus Eupator to Judas the Anointed one of Sabaoth and to the rest of the people, greetings!

Let it be known that I have issued a decree throughout all my cities and to all the peoples subjected to my rule, that they should not oppress the Judeans, but leave them to keep and to observe your law. Forgive whatever actions my father did in error, and if we have also erred, we send you Menelaos to speak to you words of peace.

Chapter 12 Notes

1 Aramaic: Byt Tr (בית תר)

This is generally accepted as an alternate spelling of Byt Swr (בית צור), the name of a town in the Judean highlands south of Jerusalem. The Greeks called it Betsoura (Βετσουρα) in the Classical era. Arabic Maccabees, which appears to be partially based on Hebrew Maccabees, also calls it Byt tr (بيت تر), although the usual Arabic spelling is byt zwr (بيت زور). Tr (תר) is almost certainly a Hebrew transliteration of the Aramaic word twr (מור), as both twr and swr, mean 'rock,' or 'flint.' The name is normalized to Beth-Zur in this translation.

Chapter 13

In those days, the Lord began to uplift the fourth kingdom, making it more powerful than the third, that is the kingdom of Rome, which was stirred up against the kingdom of Greece. The name of Rome was exalted over all the empires of the world. That was the fourth animal that Daniel, that greatly beloved man, saw in a vision. Just as that animal devoured, crushed, and trampled upon everything, so did this nation of Romans devour and crush all the other nations. They were the ones who fought with Antiochus, King of Greece, his 120 elephants, and a strong and powerful army of infantry and cavalry, whom they defeated in the battle, and forced to pay tribute to Rome.

They also humbled the pride of Hannibal,[1] the king of Africa,[2] who reigned over the city whose name was Carthage. Hannibal entered the field with an army as mighty and as numerous as the sand on the seashore. With him were all the armies of Aethiopia,[3] Cyrene, Lud, and other mighty nations. Having crossed the narrow sea between Africa and Iberia,[5] he humbled the pride of the nation of the Goths.[6] He traveled from there to the land of the Germans[7] by the Sea of Oceanus.[8] From there, he traveled to Italy and battled the Romans who went out to meet him. It was a long and fierce battle, in which the Romans were utterly routed.

However, the Romans continued to fight, and in ten years no less than eighteen battles were fought with Hannibal, but they could not make progress against him. After some time, they again gathered all their warriors, led by two valiant men, Aemilius[9] and Varro.[10] Their men assembled in battle formation by the Aufidus,[11] the battle was fought at Cannae,[12] a large city. A fierce and desperate battle was fought there in which 90,000 Romans died, including Aemilius, one of the Roman commanders. However, Varro managed to escape to Canusium,[13] a city situated between the mountains and the plain. 40,000 of Hannibal's men were killed in that battle. They followed the Romans up to the gates of the city, and he besieged the city for eight days, building turrets in front of the city, and fighting against it.

Then the Roman senators said to each other, "Let's open the gate and go and make a treaty with Hannibal, so we may live and not be put to death."

While they were discussing this, a young man named Scipio stood up, and said to the 320 senators of the city, "We can never allow ourselves to be subject to Hannibal."

"What can we do?" they answered, "We have not been able to make a stand before Hannibal for the last eighteen years?"

"Then," Scipio said, "Consider this: give me five legions of men, and I will go to the land of Africa and attack and destroy his land. As soon as Hannibal hears this, he will rush away from Rome to save his own land from my hands, and you will have peace."

After they agreed to his proposal, he took 30,000 Romans and marched to Africa, the country of Hannibal. He engaged them in battle, and Hannibal's brother Hasdrubal[14] was killed. Scipio cut off his head and brought it to Rome. He climbed the wall, and shouted to Hannibal, "Why are you so eager for our land when you can't go and save your own land from my hands, which I am destroying?"

Then he sent Hannibal his brother's head.[15] When he recognized it, he braced himself and hardened his heart, and swore not to leave the city until he had captured it, and he besieged it for several more days.

Scipio then returned to Africa and entirely devastated it. From there, he went to Carthage and besieged it. The men of Carthage sent Hannibal a letter at Rome, saying:

> Why do you desire a foreign land, when your own land is taken from you? If you will not rush back here and save us from the hand of Scipio, we will open the gate and give the city of Carthage including your palace into his hands.

CHAPTER 13

When he read this letter he wept, immediately abandoned his siege, and returned to the Aufidus, where his ships lay. He slaughtered Romans beyond counting there, and men, women, and children were taken prisoners. Then he returned to Africa with his army. Scipio went out to meet him, and a fierce war ensued between them, in which Hannibal was defeated and 50,000 of his men were killed. He was also defeated in three more pitched battles with Scipio. After that Hannibal fled to Egypt, but Scipio followed him, and Ptolemy the king turned him over to Scipio. He was taken back to Africa in great honor, and there he drank poison and died and was buried.[16] Scipio then captured the whole land of Africa, and the palace which was filled with gold and silver. From this, Rome was exalted above all the other nations.

Chapter 13 Notes

1 Hebrew: Ånybôl (אניבעל)

The person in the text is accepted as Hannibal, however, the spelling is not the correct Hebrew spelling, which is Hnybôl (חניבעל). The original Carthaginian spelling of his name was Hnbôl (𐤇𐤍𐤁𐤏𐤋), however, the the pronunciation of the Punic 𐤇 shifted from H to A by 200 AD, suggesting chapter 12 was transliterated from a Punic story sometime after 200 AD. Hannibal was a general and statesman, but not a king.

2 Hebrew: Åpryqh (אפריקה). Translation: Africa

This chapter is about the Roman conquest of Carthage, which became the Roman province of Africa, named after the Ifri people who lived there. The word ifri (ⵉⴼⵔⵉ) is Amazigh (Berber) for 'cave,' and most of the indigenous settlements in the region were built underground. The term 'Africa' was not applied to the entire continent until a few hundred years ago, and so the Aftica in the text would have been a reference to the Roman province.

3 Aramaic: Åtywpyh (אתיופיה). Translation: Aethiopia

Aethiopia (Αἰθιοπία) was the Greek name of the kingdom of Kush, but was later applied to all of Sub-Saharan Africa. The word was not used in ancient Hebrew, where Kwš (כּוּשׁ) was used. The Greek name was adopted into Aramaic, supporting an Aramaic source text.

CHAPTER 13 NOTES

4 Hebrew: Fut (פּוּט)

The Pådu (transliterated hieratic: pȝdw) were a Libyan tribe recorded in Egyptian records of the 22nd dynasty, who appear to have lived in Cyrene before the Greeks colonized the region in 631 BC. The annals of Nebuchadnezzar II report that in 567 BC, the Greeks from Putu, called the Putu Iáaman (𒀭𒆗 𒅓𒐊) in Neo-Babylonian, were fighting in the Egyptian army. The Canaanites appear to have been trading with the Pådu for centuries before the Greeks established a colony in Cyrene, and so the name Pwt (𓊪𓏲𓏏) appears to have been applied to the entire Libyan (Berber) population of northern Africa. When the Persians later conquered Egypt, Cyrene joined the Persian Empire, and they integrated Cyrene as the Satrapy of Putāya (𒋼𒀴𒐊𒈨𒐊𒀸).

5 Hebrew: Sefarad (סְפָרַד). Translation: Iberia

6 Hebrew: Gwtws (גּוֹתוֹס)

This term appears to be a transliteration of the Latin Gotus, meaning 'Goths,' which would date this chapter's Hebrew translation to after 418 AD. Between 300 and 375, the Gothic Empire dominated the Germanic tribes north of the Roman Empire. Around 375, the Huns invaded the Gothic Empire from the east, and the Goths fled south of the Danube River seeking the protection of the Byzantine legions. Although Constantinople allowed the refugees to enter Byzantine territory, they didn't provide any food or shelter, and the Goths quickly turned on the Byzantines, initiating the Gothic

War of 376 to 382. The Gothic War was followed by a civil war, in which Gothic units fought on both sides. In the early 400s, the Gothic legions united to occupy Italy, and in 418, established the Kingdom of the Goths, also called the Visigoths by the Byzantines, which dominated eastern Iberia (Spain) and southern Gaul (France). The author of this chapter is referring to Iberia as the nation of the Goths, following which they traveled west to 'Germania by the sea of Oceanus,' meaning that this chapter must have been written after 418, when the Kingdom of the Goths was established.

7 Hebrew: Grmånh (גרמאניה). Translation: Germania

The reference to the Sea of Oceanus (ים אוקינוס) indicates that this land was on the Atlantic coast west of the Kingdom of the Goths (Visigoths), which would have been the Germanic Suevian Kingdom of northwest Iberia. The Suevian Kingdom had been established in 410 after the Germanic Suebi tribe had agreed to fight for one of the sides in the Byzantine civil war. The war led to the collapse of the western half of the empire, and the Suebi occupied the province of Gallaecia, establishing their own independent kingdom.

8 Hebrew: Ym Åwqnws (ים אוקינוס). Translation: Sea of Oceanus

The Sea of Oceanus was the ancient Latin name for the Atlantic Ocean.

9 Hebrew: Åmylyws (אמיליוס). Translation: Aemilius

Lucius Aemilius Paullus was elected consul of the Roman Republic in 219 BC. He died in combat against Hannibal's forces in the Battle of Cannae that year. This was during the Second Punic War.

10 Hebrew: Wårws (ואַרוס). Translation: Varro

Gaius Terentius Varro was elected consul in 216 BC and was co-commander of the Roman forces at the Battle of Cannae, where Consul Lucius Aemilius Paullus died. The Romans elected their military commanders, and Varro, as the son of a butcher, was not the best person to lead an army. Over 40,000 Romans died on the first day of the engagement, including Aemilius, and Varro fled to the fortified city of Venusia with 4,500 troops. He later heard that a larger number of Roman survivors from the battle had amassed as Canusium, which he marched to and took command of, forming an army of around 40,000, less than half of the original size of the army that he and Aemilius had commanded.

11 Hebrew: Ååwpydws (אאופידוס). Translation: Aufidus

Aufidus was the ancient name of the Ofanto in southeast Italy. Battle of Cannae was fought between Rome and Carthage on August 2, 216 BC, at the town of Cannae, on the Aufidus River.

CHAPTER 13 NOTES

12 Hebrew: Qnwsi (קנוסי)

Battle of Cannae was fought between Rome and Carthage on August 2, 216 BC, at the town of Cannae, on the Aufidus River, in southeast Italy. Rome lost around 90,000 troops was at Cannae. After regrouping at Canusium, Varro returned to Rome.

13 Hebrew: Knwsyah (כנוסיאה). Translation: Canusium

The Roman forces regrouped at Canusium after the devastating loss at the Battle of Cannae.

14 Hebrew: Ôstrwbôl (עסתרובעל)

Hannibal's brother Ôzrbôl bn Brq (𐤐𐤓𐤒 𐤏𐤁 𐤋𐤏𐤆𐤓𐤕𐤏) was a general in the Carthaginian army, however, he died 5 years before Scipio invaded Africa. The initial defense of Carthage was led by Ôzrbôl bn Grśkn (𐤍𐤊𐤔𐤓𐤂 𐤏𐤁 𐤋𐤏𐤆𐤓𐤕𐤏), known as Hasdrubal Gisco in Latin. He committed suicide shortly after Scipio defeated him.

Hannibal and his other brother Mgw bn Brq (𐤐𐤓𐤒 𐤏𐤁 𐤅𐤂𐤌), known in Latin as Mago Barca, returned from Italy with their armies to defend Carthage. Historians debate what happened to Mago, with most accepting the Roman historian Livy's account, recorded in the 1st century AD, that Mago died at sea before reaching Africa. Conversely, the earlier Roman historian Cornelius Nepos, writing in the 1st century BC, reported that he fought in Africa, and later traveled with Hannibal until the Carthaginian senate arrested him in 193

BC. Nepos reported that after he escaped custody he later died in a shipwreck.

15 Hasdrubal's head was cut off, however, it was by Claudius Nero after the battle of Metaurus, in Italy, in 207 BC. Nero had it packed in a sack and thrown into Hannibal's camp.

16 It is unclear what the author is referring to, and may have simply been writing fiction at this point. Livy reported that 16,000 were killed in the Battle of Zama, but General Hannibal survived. He did not flee to Egypt, or take his own life, but supported the terms of Carthage's surrender before the Carthaginian Senate.

Chapter 14

The following is the contents of the letter which the Romans sent to Judas, the son of Mattathias:

Qinsius Minios, Scipio, and Menelaos, leaders of Rome, to Judas the Anointed one of Sabaoth, and to the elders of Judea greeting to you!

We have heard of your power and of your battles, and are glad, also of what Antiochus and Lysias have given you, and of what they wrote concerning the Judeans. Now we also write to ask you whether you will become our allies and friends, but not the allies of the Greeks, who have afflicted you. We are now going to war against Antioch, therefore quickly let us know who your enemies are and who your allies are.

The following is the text of the agreement made between the Romans and the Judeans:

Whether on the sea or land, whenever war is declared against the Romans, the Judeans are to assist them with all their power. They are not to supply Rome's enemies with either weapons of war or with wheat or any other food, according to the decree of the Consul and the 320 senators. If, on the other hand, war is declared against the Judeans, the Romans, in turn, are to assist the Judeans with all their power, and are not to provide the enemies of the Judeans with either weapons of war, wheat, or food of any kind. They themselves should not take any food from them unless in trouble. Further, neither party is to add or diminish what had been decreed by the Consul and the 320 senators.

CHAPTER 14

After that the land had peace for about eight months. At that time Judas began to judge his people and to weed out the wicked from his people. At that time the Judeans lived in all the cities on the sea coast from Gaza until Acre, but the Macedonian people and the people of Jaffa and Yavne caused great evil. They induced the Judeans living among them to board their ships, together with their wives and children, to go out on the sea for entertainment. The Judeans trusted them and consented to go with them, but when they arrived in the deep sea, they were thrown into the water and drowned, all 200 of them.

When Judas heard of it, he wept and proclaimed a fast. Then he rushed to Jaffa, and he besieged it, and God delivered it into his hands. After separating the Judeans, he killed the city with the edge of the sword, including the men, women, children, and babies, and burnt the city to the ground. He did the same in Yavne, and also burned the ships of both cities. The burning and smoke could be seen as far as Jerusalem, a distance of 240 stadia. In this, he avenged the blood of the women and children who were drowned in the sea. From there he traveled to the Arabian desert, killed many Arabs, and imposed a tribute upon them.

He then returned to the land of (Edom), and during the journey had to pass a certain city named Kaspin. It was very strongly fortified, for nations of all kinds lived therein. Relying upon their fortifications, they cursed Judas and called out countless slanders about Judas' people. At this, Judas exclaimed, "Oh God Sabaoth, at the sound of the trumpet You delivered the city of Jericho to the hands of Your servant Joshua. Now deliver this city into our hands, so I may avenge the insults they have cast upon the people of God."

Then, taking his shield in his left hand and unsheathing his sword, he marched bravely towards it at a very quick pace, followed by the Hasmoneans, until they reached the gate of the city. After smearing pitch on it, they placed bushes and thorns from the desert against it, and they set fire to it. It collapsed to the ground, and God delivered the city into his hands. He slaughtered so many like never had been seen before. The stream of blood that flowed from the city formed a pool like water, two stadia long and another two in width.

Chapter 15

Then they traveled a distance of 750 stadia from that place. Timothy came out to meet him with 120,000 infantry and 1,000 cavalry. After offering his prayers to God, Judas marched out against Timothy with around 10,000 chosen men. A very fierce battle followed, in which Judas slaughtered 30,000 of Timothy's army. Timothy tried to escape, but Dositheus, the commander of Judas' army, and Sosipater, a brave Israelite warrior chased him and brought him back to Judas, who ordered his head to be cut off. Timothy wept bitterly and begged him, saying, "My lord Judas, don't kill me, as there are many Judeans living in my land, and I swear that I will treat them good all the days of my life."

He took an oath, and Judas had pity upon him and did not kill him, but allowed him to go his way, and Timothy never did evil to the Judeans all the days of his life, as he kept the oath he had made.

Traveling from there, Judas marched in the direction of the wilderness and met the army of the king who had come from Arabia. He defeated them and chased them, killing another 25,000 of their men. Then he traveled to Ephron, a large city, and besieged it, and the Lord gave it into his hands. He slaughtered 20,000 in the battle.

Marching on a journey of 600 stadia, he arrived at a city named Scythopolis, and the inhabitants of

Scythopolis being very afraid of them, came out to meet them begging and crying, saying, "Oh lord, the Anointed one of Sabaoth, I beg you, ask the Judeans who live among us whether we have treated them kindly or not. Moreover, in the time of the cruel Antiochus, many Judeans escaped to us and we saved them."

The Judeans living among them testified that this was true. As soon as Judas heard this he blessed them and decided not to attack them, and he returned to Jerusalem, arriving there three days before the festival of Shavuot.

When the festival ended he marched out to Gorgios, the captain of the army of Edom, with 3,000 infantry and 4,000 cavalry. A fierce battle took place between their two armies, in which some Hasmoneans were killed. Dositheus, the commander of the army, was severely injured in the shoulders. Some of the Hasmonean warriors retreated. When Judas realized what had happened, he prayed to the Lord, encouraging his men, and rushed forward into the camp of Gorgios, slaughtering many of his men. He then shouted out, "At you, Gorgios!" He stretched out his right hand to slash him, but Gorgios dodged backward and escaped the blow. He dropped his weapons and fled. He escaped and has never been seen since. Nor was he recognized among the survivors or the dead. Some believe that he fled to the desert of Maresha, in the wilderness of Edom, and died there.

Judas returned to Edom, and after destroying all their cities, captured all the inhabitants as slaves. At this time the engraved idols of the nations were discovered under the clothes of those Hasmoneans who were killed in battle. Judas then understood that they had fallen through their iniquity, and said, "Blessed be the Lord, who discovers that which is hidden, and who revealed these secrets."

He then told the people to serve the Lord in holiness and purity and returned to Jerusalem.

Chapter 16

When Antiochus Eupator heard of all the battles Judas had waged and of the cities he had captured, he broke the covenant he had made with Judas, and marched out against him with an army as numerous as the sand upon the seashore, together with Lysias, his cousin, who also marched out at the head of a huge army. When he arrived in the land of Judea, he laid siege to Beth-Zur.

Seeing this, Judas and all the elders of Israel called upon the Lord through fasting, tears, and supplication. They also sacrificed burnt offerings and offered peace offerings. That night Judas mustered all his chosen men of the Hasmoneans, and, divided them around the camp of the king. He slaughtered 4,000 men and the largest elephant. In the morning the king organized his men in battle formation opposite Judas, and a very fierce engagement took place.

Judas suddenly noticed an elephant coated with golden armor, and as it was larger than all the other elephants, he thought the king must be riding it, and called out to his men, "Who of you are with me?"

Eleazar, one of the young Hasmoneans, immediately sprang forward and faced the elephant, knocking to the ground all who came in his way. He slashed to the right and left, and the dead fell on both sides of him. He rushed into the melee and ran in between the elephant's

legs. Then he pierced its belly with his sword, and it
collapsed upon him. He died, having sacrificed his life for
the Lord and for his people, and left a name after him,
and courage to all who heard it. It was a day of mourning
for his people. There fell in battle on that day 800 of the
king's nobles, besides the other people that were killed
among them.

The king then stopped fighting and returned to his
tent. Soon after his return, he was informed that Philip
had revolted against him and that Demetrius, the son of
Seleucus the king, was coming from Rome with a large
army, in order to take the kingdom from his hands.
Being terribly frightened, the king made peace and
made an alliance with Judas. He embraced and kissed
him, and ratified it by an oath, which Lysias joined,
saying, "We will never, as long as we live, go to war
against Jerusalem."

The king then brought out a great deal of gold from
his treasury and gave it as a gift to the temple of God in
Jerusalem. He took the Judean Menelaus as a prisoner,
who had brought Antiochus to Jerusalem to do evil, and
also Eupator. The king, being very angry with him,
ordered him to be carried up a tall tower, fifty cubits in
height, and near it, there was dust and ashes in immense
quantities. Then, he commanded his hands and feet to be
chained, and they threw him into the ash. He sank into

it and died in torment because of his thorough iniquity, he had committed many abominations before the altar of the Lord with the sacred dust and ashes. This wicked man died like this, suffocating in the very ash that he had committed the abominations. The Lord is just and repays man according to his actions and the fruit of his choices.

Chapter 17

After this, the king traveled to Macedon, and Judas judged his people, and was righteous and just. At that time, Demetrius, the son of King Seleucus, with a Roman army, engaged in battle with Antiochus Eupator, in which Antiochus and Lysias were killed, and he seized the reins of government in Antiochus in Macedon.

Alkimos the priest was a worthless man who ate pork during the reign of Antiochus, and he went to Demetrius, and said, "Long live King Demetrius! How long will you remain inactive on behalf of your servants in the land of Judea, who have fallen by the sword of Judas ben Mattathias, and his people the Judeans, who are called Hasidians? He kills us because we refuse to follow many precepts of their law."

Demetrius was stirred to anger by this, and sent Nicanor, the captain of his army, with a strong army, chariots, cavalry, elephants, and infantry beyond counting. When they arrived in Jerusalem, he sent word professing his friendship, and said, "Come and let's see each other, and consult in a friendly manner."

Judas was not afraid of any treachery and went to meet with him. When Nicanor met him, he embraced him and asked about his welfare. Seats were set up for both of them, they sat down and spoke. However, Judas had ordered his young Hasmoneans to remain armed ready for battle, in case the enemy should suddenly attack them. Therefore, his men stood near him ready at any moment for conflict, as Judas had ordered. Judas and Nicanor rose from their seats after some time and went into their respective tents, and they both remained in Jerusalem, as there was no conflict between them. On the contrary, Nicanor was very fond of Judas, and said to him, "Would it not be appropriate for a man like you to take a wife and have children?" So Judas married and fathered children.

When Alkimos recognized the admiration Judas and Nicanor had for each other, he returned to the king and informed him of what had happened. The king then sent a letter to Nicanor, saying, "If you will not send me Judas ben Mattathias shackled in chains, know that you will certainly be executed."

Judas became aware of this and left the city at night. He sounded the shofar and gave the battle signal. Then all the valiant Hasidians and Hasmoneans mustered in full force, and went to Samaria, and remained there.

In the meantime, Nicanor went to the temple of the Lord, and said to the priests, "Bring out the man who fled from me, so I can send him to the king shackled in chains."

CHAPTER 17

The priests swore to him, "He has not been here, nor have we seen him since the day before yesterday."

After hearing this, Nicanor spoke blasphemously of the temple, and spit on it. He stretched out his right hand, and pointing with his hand, said, "I will tear down this temple, and will not leave one single stone in its place, and I shall dig up and destroy all its foundations."

After this, he left in anger, and the priests went about crying between the porch and the altar, and said, "Oh God who has lived in this temple since ancient times and continues to rest here, for Your throne is here, and Your footstool is here, and all Your service. The heart of Nicanor was filled with blasphemy towards Your temple and towards Your home. He acted treacherously against the temple of Your glory and has committed abomination, therefore let him die as an abomination."

Nicanor searched all the houses of Jerusalem for Judas, and sent 500 troops to the house of Cassius,[1] the Elder of the Hasidians, who was tortured during Antiochus' reign and found perfect, for he had suffered many tortures, and was called 'Father of the Judeans and Judge in Jerusalem.'

As Nicanor was trying to show his bitter hatred of the Judeans, he sent a messenger to fetch the old man. His men surrounded the house to catch him, but the old man unsheathed his sword, pierced his bowels, and then ran up onto the wall. He jumped down at Nicanor's troops, however, they jumped back and he fell to the ground. He stood up and moved towards the troops. He stood on a large stone, and from the great loss of blood that was rapidly draining from him, he became disorientated and took part of his intestines and threw it at the troops. Then, calling upon the Lord in prayer, he died and was gathered to his people.

When Judas heard of this, he was furious and sent a message to Nicanor, saying, "Why do you delay? Come out the field, and I will show you the man you have been looking for in the chamber. Behold, he is here waiting for you in the valley and in the plain."

Nicanor then gathered all his forces and went to meet the Judeans on a Sabbath. The Judeans that were with him said, "My lord, we beg you not to act presumptuously. Grant Him honor, he who gave the Sabbath."

"Who exactly gave the Sabbath?" Nicanor asked.

"The God whose home is in the sky," they answered, "and whose dominion extends over the whole world."

Nicanor then said terrible blasphemous words that are not fit to be written down.

CHAPTER 17

Judas heard of this, and said to his men, "How long will we be indolent, and refuse to battle this reviler and blasphemer? Who is this dead dog and outcast who defies the strength and glory of Israel?"

He then marched in great anger and zeal to attack Nicanor, who came to meet him with a huge and powerful army. Judas cried to the Lord, saying, "Lord my God, You sent a messenger into the camp of Sennacherib, whose men stood up outside the city and blasphemed against You, and You destroyed his army by killing 175,000 men. The dead we counted, but the killer was not visible. Now, how much more deserving of death is this man, who has stood up against Your temple, and has blasphemed Your might and Your glory?"

On that day, a fierce and bloody battle was fought. When Judas saw Nicanor with a drawn sword, he cried out, "At you, Nicanor!" and then ran against him in the fury of his anger. Nicanor turned his back to run, but Judas grabbed hold of him and cut him in two, then dropped him to the ground. On that day, 30,000 Macedonian soldiers fell. The remainder fled but were pursued by Judas' men, who were all sounding the shofar. All the cities of Judea went out to meet the enemy and attacked them, cutting them to pieces, so that not one of them survived. Then they proceeded to strip the dead, and they found an abundance of gold, precious stones, and purple garments. They cut off Nicanor's head, and the arm that he had stretched out against God's temple, and hung them up before the gate, which has ever since, until this very day, been called 'The gate of Nicanor.' The people then rejoiced greatly, and sang the Psalms of David, King of Israel, concluding, 'For He is good, and His mercy endures forever.'

Ever since that time the Judeans celebrate this day as a feast and a holiday, on which wine is drunk on the 13th day of Adar, one day before Purim.[2] Judas judged all his people, and there was justice and righteousness in the land.

Chapter 17 Notes

1 Aramaic: dQsyaws (דקסיאוס)

The name appears to be the Aramaic spelling of 'the Cassius,' which is a Latin name. The name was omitted in Arabic Maccabees, supporting this interpretation, as Arabic Maccabees appears to have been written in Palestinian Aramaic before being translated into Arabic. The Cassius family held high positions within the Roman Republic since 502 BC when Spurius Cassius Vecellinus was elected as consul. If Cassius is not a scribal error, then it seems that the Hassidian sect was active in Italy in the 2nd century BC. If so, they are probably the source of the Vetus Latina version of Esther.

A century later, in 54 BC, a Roman general named Gaius Cassius Longinus was sent to repulse the Parthian invasion of Syria and Judea. In Arabic Maccabees, he is simply called Cassius, suggesting a connection to this earlier Cassius. It is plausible that the Cassius family in Italy was partially Judean, as many Judeans had fled into the Mediterranean Sea during the era when the Babylonians conquered Judea. General Gaius Cassius Longinus fought on the Republican side against Julius Caesar when he overthrew the Republic. Later, he and his brother Brutus assassinated Caesar, however, the combined forces of his army and the Senate were not enough to defeat Caesar's army and restore the republic.

2 This verse indicates the book is very old, as the 13th day of Adar is the Fast of Esther, not a day of feasting. The Purim holiday customs developed since the era of the *Babylonian Talmud* was compiled to include funny costumes and parades, however, this does not reflect the Purim of the Talmudic era.

The Fast of Esther is accepted as originating in Babylonia during the Geonic period, broadly dated to between 589 and 1038 AD. The Geonic period was the era that immediately followed the Talmudic era, when the Geons of the two great Babylonian Talmudic Academies interpreted the Talmud and expanded on the eras that were not clarified in the Babylonian Talmud.

In *Megillah* tractate (7b) of the *Babylonian Talmud*, the following is written regarding the Purim:

Rava said: A person is obligated to become intoxicated with wine on Purim until he is so intoxicated that he does not know how to distinguish between 'cursed is Haman' and 'blessed is Mordecai.'

There is no parallel verse in the older Jerusalem Talmud, indicating the practice had been dropped in Judea/Palestine by 200 AD. The Jewish calendar is a lunisolar calendar, and so the 13th of Adar could fall anywhere in March on the Gregorian calendar. This is essentially the same as the City Dionysia festival of the ancient Greek city-states, which took place anywhere between the 10th and 16th of Elaphêboliôn (Ἐλαφηβολιών), depending on the city-state. The Greek calendar of the era was also lunisolar, and so the Dionysia could fall anywhere in late March. Worshippers of Dionysus were also required to drink until they did not know good from evil.

The worship of Dionysus (Διονυσω) in the Temple in Jerusalem was mentioned in 2nd and 3rd Maccabees, and 2nd Maccabees as also referred to the Dionysia (Διονυσιων) being held in Jerusalem. Greek records from the era report that the God of the Judeans was Sabaoth (Σαβαώθ), who they equated with both the Greek Dionysus, and the Phrygian Sabazios (Σαβάζιος). Likewise, the early Roman records reported that the Judean God was Bacchus, the Roman equivalent of Dionysus, whose festival known as the Bacchanalia happened sometime in March before the adoption of the Julian Calendar, and then on March 17. The Bacchanalia was a festival in which worshippers of Bacchus became drunk and used various drugs. The Roman Senate became concerned about the influence the cult of Bacchus was exerting over Rome, and various political assassinations were linked to the cult. In 186 BC, the Roman Senate wrote laws to restrict the cult and merged the worship of Bacchus with the older Latin god of wine Liber Pater.

The imagery in the books of Maccabees does support the correlation between the Phrygian Sabazios (ϚΑ8ΑͰΧΟϚ) and the Judean god of the era. Sabazios was the god of the sky who rode a horse, was said to create earthquakes, and was represented by a 'hand.' Some have theorized that the god was partially based on descriptions of the Israelite god, as some Judeans were resettled in Phrygia during the Persian era. However, the Israelite God was described as riding on a 'cherub,' not a horse, and the iconography of the horse-god long predates the Judean settlement in the region. The Thracians, Trojans, and Bronze Age Greeks all worshiped a god that rode a flying horse and was said to create earthquakes. The appointment of Philip the Phrygian as the

High Preist in Jerusalem confirms that the two religions were seen as the same by many at the time.

Both Josephus and Arabic Maccabees confirm that the vineyard iconography continued to be used in the temple until shortly before the Herodian era, suggesting that Sabaoth the wine god did not disappear quickly, regardless of the redactions to the ancient scriptures that the Hasmonean dynasty made. This particular book strangely refers to Judas the Hammer as the 'Anointed of Sabaoth' many times, a term otherwise missing from ancient literature. Likewise, it refers to the Hasidians many times, a sect that is rarely mentioned in the other books. This reference to the 13th of Adar links a lost festival of the Anointed of Sabaoth with Purim, a festival originally dedicated to the god 'King' before the name 'King' was removed from the Hebrew translation of Esther.

As the Vetus Latina version of the book of Esther, which includes the name 'King,' refers to itself as the 'Book of Hadassah, which is called Esther,' this indicates the Old Latin translation was made before the Hasmonean redactors removed all references to God from Esther. The origin of the Purim festival is linked exclusively with the Book of Esther, and no other ancient Israelite or Judean text. It was mandated during the Persian era and therefore was practiced throughout the many lands that Persia ruled, so no Hasmonean redactors could have stopped the festival, however, the god 'King' was removed, likely because this was the same name as 'Molech' (מלך) in Hebrew.

In Hebrew Maccabees, Mattathias, Judas' father, both identifies his god by the title 'King' (מלך), and anoints his son in the name of Sabaoth. As no known Jewish group has ever accepted Hebrew Maccabees as a religious text, and those associated with the text reported preserving it only for historical reasons, this suggests it is quite old, possibly dating back to the Second Temple Era, when there were still Hasidians around.

Chapter 18

At the end of the year, the days of Judas came to a close, and the Lord ordained that Judas end his days, and be gathered to his people, the Hasidians. At this time Bacchides suddenly attacked Judas with 30,000 Macedonian soldiers, while he was in Laish. The 3,000 men that were with him fled like one man, and the only ones who remained were himself, his brothers, and 800 chosen men of Israel, who did not stir from their places. All these men were Judas' associates, tried veterans in all the wars that Judas had waged with the nations.

Bacchides[1] then took 15,000 men and arranged them in battle formation to the right of Judas, and to his left he placed another army of 15,000. There was a great conflict both on the right and left of Judas. When he saw the battle was very fierce, and that Bacchides stood on his right, for all the generals of Bacchides remained on the right, and that the right wing was with him, he shouted and leaped forward followed by his brothers, and the few Hasmoneans.

He ran in the direction of Bacchides, and a fierce and terrible battle followed, in which heaps of Macedonians were killed. As soon as Judas saw Bacchides standing in the middle of the people, he ran towards him in the strength of his anger and killed many of his generals. He struck out right and left at all who came in his way, slaying enemies beyond counting, until he had no place to walk except upon the dead, and he walked over the corpses.

He came face to face with Bacchides with sword unsheathed and dripping with blood. As soon as Bacchides saw Judas' face, it appeared to him like that of a lion hunting its prey, and fear and trembling seized him. He turned his back and fled in the direction of Ashdod, but Judas chased him, and killed all 15,000 of his men, with the edge of the sword.

Bacchides succeeded in escaping to Ashdod with his army, which fled behind him, and when he found Judas was tired and weary, he turned and attacked him. Bacchides came out from the city, and war was waged on every side, and many more were killed, including Judas, who fell with the others that died. His brothers Simeon and Jonathan took him and buried him on Mount Modi'in, and all of Israel mourned for him for many days. The number of years when Judas, nicknamed Maccabee, judged Israel, was six years and the Lord caused him to prosper all the days of his life.

Chapter 18 Notes

1 Aramaic: Bqydys (בקידיס).

Bacchides (Βακχίδης) was a general and governor of Syria, and advisor of King Demetrius I Soter of the Seleucid Empire. The Hebrew spelling of his name is Bqkyds (בקכידס), indicating the chapter was translated from an Aramaic text.

Also Available

ALSO AVAILABLE

- Octateuch: The Original Orit

ENOCH AND METATRON SERIES:
- Books of Enoch Collection

- Books of Enoch and Metatron Collection

- Books of Metatron Collection

- Secrets of Enoch

OTHER TRANSLATIONS:
- Apocalypses of Ezra

- Arabic Maccabees

- Life of Adam and Eve

- Memories of the New Kingdom

- Septuagint's Esther and the Vetus Latina Esther

- Septuagint's Ezekiel and the Ba'al Cycle

- Septuagint's Job and the Testament of Job

- Septuagint's Proverbs and the Wisdom of Amenemope

- The Amarna Letters

- Testaments of the Patriarchs Collection

- Tobit and Ahikar

- Ugaritic Texts: Ba'al Cycle

- Wisdom of Ahikar

www.ingramcontent.com/pod-product-compliance
Lightning Source LLC
Chambersburg PA
CBHW071151120626
46546CB00006B/2219